Praise for
Dancing in the Rain

"*Dancing in the Rain* compellingly makes the case for being fully present, leaning in, and living one's values. This book is such a gift for educational leaders."

> —**Ari Betof**, head of school, Boston University Academy, and lecturer,
> University of Pennsylvania Graduate School of Education

"Informed by rich experience and wise discernment, this practical and inspiring book leads educators to seamlessly combine their outer lives of service with the inner life of contemplation. Murphy has brilliantly translated contemplative principles and practices into the language of education and leadership."

> —**Mirabai Bush**, senior fellow, Center for Contemplative
> Mind in Society, and author, *Contemplative Practices in Higher
> Education: Powerful Methods to Transform Teaching and Learning*

"For years, I struggled with the demands of being a principal while caring for my mother with Alzheimer's. On the outside, I appeared all together, while the real me struggled in silence. No one ever told me to care for myself—until this life-changing book. I'm no Beyoncé, but I'm learning to dance in the rain."

> —**Karen Marie Byron-Johnson**, principal,
> Whitney M. Young Leadership Academy, Cleveland, Ohio

"The superintendent has one of the most difficult jobs in America. Jerry Murphy provides practical and thoughtful advice on how to effectively address the critical challenges school district leaders face on an everyday basis."

> —**Daniel A. Domenech**, executive director, AASA
> The Schoo

D1115357

"This kind book takes the core of what we are learning in the science of acceptance, self-compassion, mindfulness, and values and gently puts it in the hands of the reader, one key feature at a time. There is a way that things work—personally and in our leadership roles. The core of it has been known in our wisdom traditions for eons, but in the modern world we need it to be simplified, tested, and made relevant and accessible. This book does exactly that. Highly recommended."

—**Steven C. Hayes**, codeveloper of Acceptance and Commitment Therapy, and author, *Get Out of Your Mind and Into Your Life: The New Acceptance and Commitment Therapy*

"Dean Jerome Murphy provides an invaluable, lyrical, and extremely practical guide for all who seek to lead with wisdom. He even shows hard-charging people how to enjoy the fruits of their labor! *Dancing in the Rain* is a fabulous, richly useful book."

—**Ronald Heifetz**, founding director, Center for Public Leadership, and King Hussein bin Talal Senior Lecturer in Public Leadership, Harvard Kennedy School

"*Dancing in the Rain* takes a fresh look at leadership and its challenges. Peppered with real-life stories, the book chronicles Murphy's own transformation as he learned to apply mindfulness and self-compassion to his leadership. His stories will help you align your work with your values, slow down and be present with the ups and downs of your work, take time to nourish yourself and learn to safely express your emotions with authenticity. It is a must-read for anyone in a leadership position."

—**Patricia A. Jennings**, associate professor, University of Virginia, and author, *Mindfulness for Teachers: Simple Skills for Peace and Productivity in the Classroom*

"A wise distillation of deep insights and practices which, if implemented, will go far to transforming lives and organizations, and thus, the world."

—**Jon Kabat-Zinn**, author, *Coming to Our Senses: Healing Ourselves and the World Through Mindfulness*

"Practical and wise. Doing the exercises will help you unstress and lead with understanding and heart."

—**Jack Kornfield**, author, *A Path with Heart: A Guide Through the Perils and Promises of Spiritual Life*

"I wish that the gentle wisdom and guidance that *Dancing in the Rain* provides had been available to me sooner. I highly recommend this book for leaders who wish to lead in soulful and mindful ways; for leaders who dare to go inward in ways that help inform their outer work in the world. May this help them flourish and thrive."

—**Linda Lantieri**, cofounder and senior program advisor, Collaborative for Academic, Social, and Emotional Learning (CASEL)

"Rich with anecdotes from his own experience as dean of the Harvard Graduate School of Education, this wise new book on mindful leadership explores the common mental traps of leading educational organizations: our resistances and our tendencies to ruminate and rebuke ourselves. Murphy then offers compassionate guidance, and dozens of exercises, in his own heartfelt voice, about coming back to center and being in the 'dance.' A lovely and accessible book for educational leaders."

—**Kirsten Olson**, coauthor, *The Mindful School Leader: Practices to Transform Your Leadership and School*

"In this compassionate and wise book, Murphy shares years of experience as an educator, manager, and leader. He examines both the internal and external burdens of leadership as well as skillful ways to stay focused and kind to both oneself and others. He writes as if he were talking with the reader over a cup of coffee. But, his ideas are fresh and psychologically sophisticated. This is a must-read book for leaders, administrators, and anyone who has a position of authority and visibility."

—**Mary Pipher**, author of *Reviving Ophelia: Saving the Selves of Adolescent Girls*

"Essential reading for education leaders and administrators—a wise, compassionate, open-hearted guide to leading with insight and care. Jerry Murphy offers a sophisticated yet simple and accessible distillation of principles that will benefit others immeasurably."

—**Lizabeth Roemer**, professor of psychology, University of Massachusetts Boston, and coauthor, *Worry Less, Live More: The Mindful Way through Anxiety Workbook*

"*Dancing in the Rain* is a welcome contribution to the world of education. Here is a practical set of tools that educational leaders can call on for support and strength in challenging times. The stresses of leadership don't seem likely to lessen—what good fortune that the skills for handling such stress are becoming more widely available."

—**Sharon Salzberg**, author, *Lovingkindness: The Revolutionary Art of Happiness* and *Real Happiness: The Power of Meditation*

"*Dancing in the Rain* is a gift for school leaders. Jerry Murphy's wisdom, humor, and humility shine through every page, reflecting his own leadership journey. It's a vital resource, including a toolkit of exercises and practices that support leaders in navigating variable weather patterns while still enjoying the dance."

—**Pamela Seigle**, executive director, Courage & Renewal Northeast, Wellesley College

"For every educator daring to lead in these daunting times, here is an honest, helpful, and hopeful book on how to do it with mind and heart from one who has seen it, taught it, done it—danced it—and lived to tell the tale."

—**Diana Chapman Walsh**, president emerita, Wellesley College

"Exercising leadership in public education is like managing the Boston Red Sox—everyone tells us how to do our job. Murphy sees us as human beings grappling with difficult jobs, and compassionately offers practical insights on how to take care of ourselves while we are busy taking care of everyone else. An absorbing book, a must-read for administrators."

—**Jeffrey M. Young**, superintendent of schools, Cambridge, MA Public Schools

Dancing
in the Rain

Dancing in the Rain

Leading with Compassion, Vitality, and Mindfulness in Education

Jerome T. Murphy

HARVARD EDUCATION PRESS
Cambridge, Massachusetts

Paperback ISBN 978-1-61250-962-4
Library Edition ISBN 978-1-61250-963-1

Library of Congress Cataloging-in-Publication Data

Names: Murphy, Jerome T.
Title: Dancing in the rain : leading with compassion, vitality, and
    mindfulness in education / Jerome T. Murphy.
Description: Cambridge, Massachusetts : Harvard Education Press, [2016] |
    Includes bibliographical references and index.
Identifiers: LCCN 2016014317 | ISBN 9781612509624 (pbk.) | ISBN 9781612509631
    (library edition)
Subjects: LCSH: Reflective teaching. | Teaching—Philosophy. | Educational
    leadership. | Mindfulness (Psychology). | Holistic education.
Classification: LCC LB1025.3 .M875 2016 | DDC 371.14/4—dc23
LC record available at https://lccn.loc.gov/2016014317

Published by Harvard Education Press,
an imprint of the Harvard Education Publishing Group

Harvard Education Press
8 Story Street
Cambridge, MA 02138

Cover Design: Wilcox Design
Cover Photo: iStock.com/keanu2
The typefaces used in this book are Joanna Nova and TT Prosto Sans.

For all the committed educators
who dare to lead in stressful times

CONTENTS

CONTENTS

CONTENTS

FOREWORD

"LIKE IT OR NOT, there's no leading without bleeding." These words, coming from Jerry Murphy, former dean of the Graduate School of Education at Harvard University, may actually evoke a sigh of relief among people in leadership positions. You mean *all* leaders go through tough times and it's not just me? You mean it's not a personal flaw when my staff doesn't agree with me, my colleagues don't honor my achievements, and I'm exhausted at the end of the day? Can I be an excellent leader without hearing the constant hum of self-criticism in the back of my mind and constantly worrying that things will go wrong?

Incessant fear and self-criticism are not our fault, but they are our responsibility. Human beings are finely tuned to respond to threat—the fight-or-flight-or-freeze response—since the days of the saber-toothed tiger. But what happens when our threats are mostly *internal*, for example, when we struggle with common human emotions like fear, anger, or shame? That's when we tend to make our lives more difficult. Jerry Murphy identified our most common reactions as the *three Rs*—resisting, ruminating, and rebuking ourselves—hardly the state of mind we wish to bring to leadership.

An apt metaphor is the ancient tale of two arrows: When we're shot by an arrow, we naturally feel pain. Soon afterward, however, we begin to grieve, worry, and blame ourselves for our misfortune: "Why me? Why did this happen to me?" These reactions are akin to shooting ourselves with a second arrow. The suffering of the second arrow may sometimes last longer and be more intense than that of the first arrow. Just consider how long it may have taken you to fall sleep after someone at work questioned how you were doing your job. Fortunately, we can bring a variety of inner skills to bear on these inner threats, as Jerry Murphy offers in this book. These skills allow us not only to tolerate and transform adversity, but even to thrive in the midst of it—to dance in the rain.

Was there ever a time in your career when you just wanted to sit down with a wise and compassionate colleague and discuss the challenges of leadership in an open and honest way, without an agenda? This book captures the generosity of such an encounter. With candid and often quite touching anecdotes from his personal life and his distinguished career in education, Murphy conveys in simple language what every leader needs to know to succeed with heartfulness at the highest levels of leadership. His simple acronym—MY DANCE—distills the essence of newly emerging fields of scientific psychology, including human values, mindfulness, experiential acceptance, savoring, self-compassion, and wisdom studies. Rather than burdening the reader with too much information, Murphy digests this body of knowledge for us and presents it in an intimate manner that leaves the reader feeling both empowered and comforted.

The real promise of this book lies in creating a bridge between reading and cultivating new mental habits in daily life. Burgeoning research over the past twenty years has shown that the daily practice of mindfulness, acceptance, and compassion can alter the structure and function of our brains and affect our lives for the better. Mindfulness alone has been shown to enhance overall life satisfaction and happiness, improve physical and mental health, enrich personal relationships, and develop healthy habits like diet and exercise, and reduce occupational burnout. All the skills that Murphy has selected for this book reflect key psychological processes that underlie healthy psychological functioning and emotional resilience.

Research suggests that the degree of benefit we derive from practicing skills like mindfulness depends on how much we practice. But who has time to practice? Fortunately, most of the skills suggested in this book can be practiced in the midst of a busy day when we take just a few minutes to breathe, to explore how we're feeling, or to offer ourselves some encouragement or kindness when things get rough. Sometimes, all we need is a moment to remind ourselves what really matters in our lives, to reset the compass to our deepest values.

This book is really about doing less, not more—less resisting, less ruminating, and less rebuking ourselves for not measuring up. It offers the possibility that we can still thrive as leaders by allowing ourselves to be more fully human and, in doing so, to extend the same generosity to others.

Christopher Germer
Author, *The Mindful Path to Self-Compassion*
Lecturer on Psychology, Part-time
Harvard Medical School

Introduction

Man was made for Joy & Woe
And when this we rightly know
Thro the World we safely go
                    —*William Blake*

ONE AUTUMN DAY, I spotted this droll poster tacked to the office wall of a seasoned leader at a state department of education:

—— NOTICE ——

The objective of all dedicated department employees should be to thoroughly analyze all situations, anticipate all problems prior to their occurrence, have answers for these problems, and move swiftly to solve these problems when called upon . . .

However . . .

When you are up to your ass in alligators, it is difficult to remind yourself that your original objective was to drain the swamp.

Sound familiar? In fact, do you ever find yourself bogged down in difficulties, fretting about expectations, or just plain swamped by the biting stress of leadership?

If so, you are not alone. Nearly half of school principals report being under great stress, and 75 percent feel their job has become too complex, says a 2013 MetLife Survey.[1] Indeed, there are "so many pressures crushing administrators today," a school principal recently wrote me, "it is enough for many to question why they made the decision to come out of the classroom in the first place."

A similar point is made by Paul Ash, a central office administrator for thirty-six years, who has spent the last ten as superintendent of the Lexington Public Schools in Massachusetts. In a note to me, he describes in stark language the stress and emotional impact of dealing with the relentless pressures facing education leaders today: "Superintendents often feel like they're going to be 'killed' by conflicts caused by parents, school boards, teachers, unions, and media. In fact, the English word 'leadership' originates in the ancient root 'leith,' which meant 'to go forth and die,' as in battle. While superintendents are not expected to launch actual life-threatening battles, it often feels this way when they're at the center of intense conflicts that could cost them their reputation or employment." Talk about snapping alligators.

It seems like leaders today live in what the US Army calls a VUCCA world—one marked by volatility, uncertainty, complexity, chaos, and ambiguity—with unyielding pressures to work harder, longer, and smarter and to do more with less. To make things worse, few venues exist to honestly discuss such topics as fear, anger, shame, loneliness, isolation, self-doubt, or feeling unappreciated. Little wonder many leaders are stressed out—and in their whimsical moments might dream about creating a new app, Stress Toys "R" Us.

We all yearn to flourish in these stressful times, and scientific studies show that a modicum of stress actually enhances performance.[2] But the unwelcome truth is that leaders often experience their work as emotionally painful and draining, even if they don't want to admit it. No matter what form it takes—frustration, regret, anxiety, shame, exhaustion, self-doubt, isolation, hurt, depression, you name it—emotional discomfort is an inevitable feature of leadership work today. I should know. I've been there—and have learned firsthand the hard fact: like it or not, there's no leading without bleeding.

Not surprisingly, we dislike the emotional discomfort triggered by our stressful circumstances, which we believe lie at the root of our difficulties. It turns out, however, that outside pressures are often not the chief problem, as counterintuitive as that may sound. Instead, a big threat to flourishing as a leader comes from responding unskillfully to the internal stress of leadership, which can turn inevitable discomfort into debilitating anguish.

As we will see, leaders respond unskillfully mainly by (1) ruminating excessively over upsets, (2) resisting discomfort and trying to escape it, and (3) rebuking themselves for falling short. In chapter 2, I explain how these three ways of responding can aggravate everyday discomfort and turn it into mind-made misery, which can in turn undermine leadership work. In the face of pressure, we often react rashly, sidetrack our work, forget to nourish ourselves, and lose sight of what really matters to us. All too often, our effectiveness deteriorates, our joy evaporates, our energy dissipates—and far too many leaders become dispirited and tune out, bow out, or burn out.

If this pattern ever rings true for you, there's good news. Everyday discomfort may be inevitable, but mind-made misery is avoidable. You can learn how to constructively handle the pressures and discomfort you encounter without making them worse. Indeed, leadership work need not be as hard as it often is.

What's more, you can actually flourish. Even in a pressure-cooker world, you can be at your best, living life fully with grace and zest as a high-performing leader. You can learn to lead without going off the rails every time you feel overwhelmed. Indeed, you can learn to take stress more in stride, make wiser choices, and retain your sense of humor. You can seize the wonderful opportunities that leadership work provides and live a life that embodies meaning and vitality. This book aims to start you on this journey.[3]

WHAT THIS BOOK IS ABOUT

Given my spotlight on flourishing, you may be wondering what flourishing has to do with being an effective leader. Building on The Free Dictionary definition—"to fare well"—I believe the meaning is aptly captured in the metaphor of dancing in the rain, an image intended to convey an upbeat, and realistic, way of leading and living in stressful times.

For those old-timers who recall a giddy-with-love Gene Kelly dancing through puddles in the delightful movie Singin' in the Rain, alas, his trouble-free circumstances aren't exactly what leaders encounter. Instead, by rain, I mean that stressful upsets, like storms, are an inevitable feature of leading and living on earth. We may not like stormy weather, but it is here to stay whether we want it or not—it's OK to get wet. Rain further implies that we humans usually try to escape life's storms by raising an umbrella or running for cover. Such strategies work with real rain, but when we try to escape our feelings, as we will see, we can drown in them.

The metaphor of rain also suggests that troubling thoughts and feelings are often like summer squalls, which have various durations and levels of intensity. And the metaphor suggests that sometimes what we experience as difficult and unpleasant can also be a surprising gift. Just as rain is vital for seeds to sprout, emotional pain can foster personal growth and creativity by motivating us to look inside ourselves and do things that otherwise we wouldn't consider.

Dancing implies taking action. It is the very opposite of being off somewhere lost in our heads, just fretting over the rain in our lives. And dancing means engaging wholeheartedly in different kinds of activities that make us come fully alive: action inspired by our values, which fosters a sense of meaning, purpose, and vitality; mindfulness practices, which develop peace of mind, presence, and perspective; and other nourishing activities that soothe our souls by bringing a sense of joy, satisfaction, and accomplishment.

Dancing further implies getting out of our way and being fully present with all our senses—in step with the music, in synch with the changing beat. And dancing implies action marked by skill and grace. You may be feeling bad because of the rain in your life, but you still can take action that makes you come alive. And as a bonus, you can make yourself feel better in the process.

Dancing in the rain stands for living life fully, especially in the midst of life's storms, and it entails a number of things:

- a new way to respond to our difficulties, *being with* them instead of *being* them, which reduces their hold on us and opens us to the joy of being fully present and engaged
- a conscious choice to be guided by our core values, rather than meandering through life whipsawed by upsetting circumstances and at the mercy of our inhibitions
- a willingness to stand up and dance even when we are unmotivated to do so, on the theory that we can change how we feel by changing what we do
- a recognition that sometimes—often—we'll encounter setbacks because heavy downpours will divert us from our priorities

At its core, dancing in the rain is a way of being, a way of flourishing as a leader—and as a human being—in a world brimming with sunny skies and gloomy storms, a buoyant and constructive way of leading and living, which you can learn and put into practice, at least some of the time.

What's more, the capacity to dance in the rain is central to *sustained* effectiveness in today's world. After all, it's hard enough to find able educators willing to take on leadership tasks, but an even harder job is identifying promising leaders with the motivation and skills to handle the challenges without losing their edge or throwing in the towel. And beyond the benefits of sustained effectiveness, the perception that a leader is dancing in the rain can directly enhance organizational productivity. A display of vitality in the face of challenges, for example, can be inspiring and energizing—it sets an infectious tone that motivates others to perform at high levels.

Most important, I prize dancing in the rain because this way of leading frees us from preoccupation with our difficulties and helps us cultivate the inner strength to look outward to serve others effectively and to promote broader issues of justice. This is no easy task, say Dan Edwards and his coauthors at the Center for Contemplative Mind in Society: "Burnout is a growing trend in the social justice community and one of the most difficult challenges we confront . . . [T]he best way to sustain ourselves while working for change is with the help of contemplative practices: activities that, when incorporated into our daily life, bring us strength, peace, and inspiration."[4]

Donald Rothberg, a meditation teacher, echoes this point of view:

> Those of us who aim to transform both ourselves and the world come under heavy pressure, both from outside and inside, that make[s] it very challenging to take care of ourselves and the world over the long haul . . . [T]he inner difficulties are perhaps more daunting than the outer difficulties, for they can paralyze and end our engagement. We must somehow sustain ourselves over a lifetime and work with and through such challenges as burnout, despair and

hopelessness, fear, an often burning anger at injustice . . . and a sense of being overwhelmed by pain and suffering.[5]

And as the well-known meditation teacher Matthieu Ricard reminds us, the "ultimate reason" for doing this work is to "transform ourselves in order to transform the world." He adds, "We transform ourselves so we can become better human beings and serve others in a wiser and more effective way."[6]

Taken together, the various aspects of learning to dance in the rain facilitate focused attention and engagement, sustained productivity and effectiveness, and service to others—and lie at the heart of just plain living the way many of us want to live.

WHOM THIS BOOK IS FOR

This book is aimed mainly at top education leaders and those aspiring to these positions, at all levels of education—school principals, district superintendents, college deans, university presidents, and other administrators. It is especially aimed at high-functioning leaders who want to enhance their inner strengths so that they can better lead and flourish in a stress-filled world.

The book is also aimed at those who prepare education leaders in schools of education and elsewhere. With a few exceptions, strikingly little attention is paid to how leaders should deal with emotional upheavals at work. Indeed, the usual message is to ignore your feelings—keep a stiff upper lip and soldier on—shortsighted advice.

In addition, the perspectives and practices presented in this book are sufficiently universal to hold lessons for others beyond those in high-level education posts. Officials in nonprofit organizations, government, and even for-profit businesses are likewise wrestling with the nonstop demands of a turbulent world. Moreover, teachers, counselors, caregivers, and others who may not formally head organizations, but who do act as informal leaders in complex and difficult settings, face challenges in mobilizing people to make good things happen. Finally, this book is aimed at a general audience—all of us ordinary mortals who long to flourish and live effective lives that matter in the face of common obstacles.

FILLING A GAP

I have written this book—a primer, if you will—to help fill a large gap in the education leadership literature, namely, the need for a succinct and user-friendly guide that addresses the inner lives of busy leaders and how they can better lead and live in difficult jobs. This volume grows out of my personal experiences as a dean at the Harvard Graduate School of Education; my years teaching leadership courses; lucky—and not so lucky—circumstances that have forever changed my research, my teaching, and my life; and some recent workshops that have helped me develop and test-drive many of the ideas presented here. I also share a few personal experiences that especially help the reader see tangible examples of the everyday stress in leadership.

This book introduces seven concrete steps to flourishing as a leader, a framework whose acronym is MY DANCE (see the box "Seven Steps of MY DANCE"). The seven steps, introduced in chapter 3, are intended to supplement the important work on the external lives of leaders—work that I and others have addressed elsewhere, with its focus on organizational, political, and interpersonal skills. The exercises interspersed in the discussion of MY DANCE can be used to cultivate inner strengths directly tied to the effectiveness of leaders: clear thinking, focused attention, steadiness under fire, resilience, and a broad perspective, to name just a few.

I've also written this book to complement the emergent—and inspiring—new literature linking mindfulness and leadership.[7] I, too, emphasize the importance of being mindful, as defined by Jon Kabat-Zinn, a pioneer in bringing meditation to the West: "Mindfulness," he explains in his popular formulation,

Seven Steps of MY DANCE

Mind your values: Take action inspired by what matters most to you, so that you can live a vital and meaningful life instead of getting sidetracked by upsets or just drifting along without a sense of purpose.

Yield to now: Slow down and focus your attention on the present moment so that you can be fully engaged, balanced, and even joyful instead of racing through life on autopilot and ruminating about the past and the future.

Disentangle from upsets: Mentally step back, observing and making room for upsets so that you can gain the perspective needed to constructively handle upsets instead of overidentifying with them, which can make things worse.

Allow unease: Open up to upsets even if you dislike them. In this way, you can wisely embrace what is already here and you can pursue your values instead of resisting discomfort in a futile attempt to escape your inner reality.

Nourish yourself: Engage in everyday activities designed to replenish your energy, restore your perspective, and revitalize your sense of well-being instead of depleting your reserves.

Cherish self-compassion: Give yourself the kindness you need and deserve instead of rebuking yourself for your shortcomings, so that you can enhance your resilience and reach out to others with compassion.

Express feelings wisely: Carefully reveal your human side to build trusting relationships instead of damaging your credibility by lurching between reacting rashly and concealing any hint of feelings.

"is awareness, cultivated by paying attention in a sustained and particular way: on purpose, in the present moment, and non-judgmentally."[8]

Mindfulness can be helpful in calming the mind, maintaining focus, making clear and wise decisions, and dealing with stress—among other benefits that scientists are beginning to document. Indeed, the cover story in the November 2014 issue of *Scientific American* sets out the growing neuroscientific evidence that meditation makes a difference:

> When we learn how to juggle or play a musical instrument, the brain undergoes changes through a process called neuroplasticity. A brain region that controls the movement of a violinist's fingers becomes progressively larger with mastery of the instrument. A similar process appears to happen when we meditate. Nothing changes in the surrounding environment, but the meditator regulates mental states to achieve a form of inner enrichment ... [R]esearch has begun to show that meditation can rewire brain circuits to produce salutary effects not just on the mind and the brain but on the entire body.[9]

But this is not just a book about mindfulness. Indeed, I draw on a wide range of related methods that help us build the skills needed for establishing our own sense of meaning and purpose in leadership, for self-compassion, for creating everyday nourishing activities, and for expressing emotions wisely in public.

My aim is to help leaders help themselves flourish in these stressful times and in turn improve their effectiveness, thereby enhancing the quality of education. To this end, I distill perspectives and practices from modern psychology and ancient wisdom traditions and draw on personal lessons from work and home. The impediments to flourishing are not just the outside pressures we face, but also how we respond to them inside ourselves. All too often, we become prisoners of self-defeating habits that undermine our effectiveness, cause needless suffering for us and others, and sidetrack what gives life a sense of purpose.

In emphasizing our internal responses to external pressures, I am decidedly not suggesting that leaders simply roll over and play dead in the face of pressures inappropriately imposed upon them—for example, conditions that result from unfair school-finance laws. Rather, educators need to develop the internal skills and wisdom to play the cards they are dealt when necessary, while simultaneously looking for openings to create a more supportive and just work environment.

Few complex problems have one-size-fits-all solutions. But the seven steps of MY DANCE can give you a variety of approaches for tackling many everyday leadership challenges. The book offers ways to help you act on what matters most to you, tune into the present moment, take setbacks less personally, and nourish yourself frequently. You can learn how to share your emotions wisely and how to dodge three unhelpful Rs: resisting reality, ruminating unduly, and rebuking yourself for falling short. With practice and persistence, you too can advance toward dancing in the rain as an effective leader.

I write not as a psychologist, brain scientist, Buddhist, or coach, but as a lifelong teacher and veteran leader committed to social justice and education reform. I know firsthand both the upheavals of leading and the benefits of practicing the steps developed in this book. As a synthesizer, I also write as a bricoleur, putting together approaches with whatever resources are available to me at the time.

Taken together, some ten years of inquiry, both professional and personal, has resulted in this progress report on an unexpected adventure. Earlier in my life, I never could have imagined taking this illuminating voyage to a completely new territory and writing a book—and I know I still have so much more to learn. For now, I hope these efforts are helpful as you ponder how to lead and live in stressful times.

Drowning in the Rain

The Difficulties of Leadership

It's hard to lead a cavalry charge if you
think you look funny on a horse.

—*Adlai Stevenson II*

MY EXPERIENCES AS DEAN

Although I didn't know it at the time, the seed for this book was planted in 1982, when I became the new associate dean of the Harvard Graduate School of Education, working with the also-new dean Patricia Albjerg Graham. (When asked, I merrily described my job as a mouse training to be a rat; later I became the chief rat—dean—at the school for nine years.) Back then, Harvard's various schools were fiercely independent, with vast differences in resources and with limited oversight from the sparsely staffed central university; the infelicitous phrase was "every tub on its own bottom." Blessed with copious freedom from bosses and ever mindful of a powerful (and wonderful) faculty, Pat and I "ran" the school with the help of a small cadre of dedicated administrators.

Looking back, my "deaning" days were deeply fulfilling—and enjoyable—for half a dozen reasons. The work provided an opportunity to strive toward many goals:

- make a difference on a big stage, as I worked with others to try to put ambitious dreams into action
- grow personally by developing new skills—e.g., learning to wing it—in response to an avalanche of new demands on my time
- broaden my perspective and develop a wider worldview by working with a range of people from both inside and outside the field of education
- show up for individuals at times of greatest vulnerability—e.g., at moments of sickness and death, of doubt and failure—and show up at moments of celebration
- experience exhilaration from working with a team of dedicated colleagues and students taking steps toward building an organization I love
- get rich, not through lots of money, of course, but through the richness of spirit that comes from being of service to others, as I would remind my students

What's more, I had a lot of fun stepping back and observing the human interplay at Harvard. It was a kick, for example, to watch the dance of deans in our monthly meetings with Harvard's president, as we all sometimes acted like peacocks displaying our feathers, competing for power and attention.

Because of all these rewards, being a Harvard dean for seventeen years was a highlight of my career, turning me into an unabashed advocate of leadership work and the joy it can bring. At the same time, I also found the everyday reality of leadership to be somewhat different—and personally harder—than I had expected. When I started, I was aware of the complexity of organizational life from my previous work and research, but I nonetheless expected that much of my time and energy would be spent on the high-minded aspects of leading. Early on, however, I was abruptly brought down to earth by a fellow faculty member who, in the midst of a lofty conversation about the school's direction, suddenly blinked and asked, "What are you going to do about the odor strips?" Sensing my confusion, he pressed on. "I'm allergic to the new odor strips in the fourth-floor bathroom, and something needs to be done!" I expressed concern and promised to have the problem fixed.

I also learned that it was much harder to navigate the rocky terrain of leadership than I expected; I was sometimes pushed outside my comfort zone. It was not the messiness of the work, the continuous problems, or the intellectual challenges. If anything, it was invigorating to try to find clever solutions to daily problems where there appeared to be no good ways to move forward. Rather, the work was difficult for me mainly because of the emotional challenges: the weight of expectations attached to working at Harvard; personal tendencies to seek perfection and to fret; and the burden of hiding my inner tension for fear of looking weak in front of my colleagues—and letting them down. I don't think I came close to burning out, but I often felt overwhelmed and exhausted.

While I knew that I was often overwrought, I didn't know if that was normal for this line of work or if something was wrong with me—or if I could do anything about it. At the suggestion of a trusted colleague, I hired an organizational consultant, who turned out to be invaluable. For several years, I met with Barry Jentz at my home every six weeks or so for two hours. We talked about management issues—how to chair faculty meetings, how to build trust, how to fire a staff member effectively and humanely when there was no other option. But mostly we talked about what was really bugging me at the time—frustration with a faculty member, exasperation with Harvard's inequality, my feeling stupid for a dumb quote in the newspaper, feeling like a fraud for not knowing how to fix the public schools, and so on. Each time we met, it felt like Barry gave me a new lease on life.

Overall, I learned from these experiences that leadership is a highly complex activity that has little to do with being a bigger-than-life boss with all the answers. Yes, dreams can be realized and the work can be deeply rewarding, but a leader must learn how to navigate the daily difficulties and emotional tangles of the work.

COMMON EMOTIONAL TANGLES

Ordinary life can be filled with excitement and joy—and it can also be filled, as we all know, with pain and suffering: the loss of a parent, a devastating illness, an unexpected divorce, disturbing memories about growing up, worries about college bills, a sense of helplessness in controlling our destiny. Each of us has a different list of challenges, and our lists go on and on. Experiencing emotional difficulties—and finding the means to handle the pain—are fundamental parts of being human. "It is not something to be ashamed of, nor a sign of weakness, and not a reflection of inner failing," says psychiatrist Mark Epstein. "It is simply a fact of life."[1]

In my experience, the all-too-familiar stresses of ordinary life are multiplied and magnified in high-stakes leadership positions. For one thing, ordinary mortals don't check their feelings at the office door—the workplace is a second home for many leaders, and their workmates are their second families. For another, the responsibilities of leadership present significant new sources of difficulty, and these sources are exacerbated because moments of difficulty are often played out in public, thereby making leaders more vulnerable to criticism and embarrassment—and a flood of innuendo and rumors. To boot, if there's a local issue, it can easily go global because of social media; these days, everyone seems to have a strong opinion, often cutting and mean, about how shoddily you're doing your job.

If leadership is difficult in general, it may be even harder in the public sector, especially those jobs involving children, "the most precious jewel for most people," Jeffrey Young, the super-intendent of Cambridge Public Schools in Massachusetts, told me. "You don't get a second chance at fourth grade; you just can't do experiments with people's sons and daughters. The stakes are too high, immediate, and, by parents' perceptions, permanent." Young believes the "burden of leadership is already great enough, but when it involves young children, the decisions become more enduring and heavy. 'What if my policy ruins some kids' lives?'" These sentiments were echoed in a recent speech at Harvard by Jennifer Cheatham, superintendent of the Madison Metropol-itan School District in Wisconsin. Being a superintendent, she said, is "inherently emotional work. It's about children."[2]

This emotional dimension of leadership is also prevalent in the private sector, as documented by business professor Linda Hill in the lives of first-time managers. The new professionals describe their initial year in their new job as a period of surpris-ing emotional upheaval—more debilitating and overwhelming than they had ever imagined. Some "spoke of insomnia, low-grade headaches, back pain, and increased arguments." One con-fided, "I never knew a promotion could be so painful."[3]

While a new management job can be particularly stressful, Hill contends that the roots of leadership discomfort grow out of four enduring features of managerial work. There is the "role strain" caused by the overload, uncertainty, and conflict. Lead-ers also face the drumbeat of negativity resulting from problems constantly dumped on their desk. The isolation of authority is another stress. ("I'm no longer one of the boys," said one man-ager. "No one asks me out for lunch. No one gossips with me. I'm alone.") Then there are the other "burdens of leadership"—thorny trade-offs and the weight of being a role model and wielding power over people's lives.[4]

In the same vein, Rick Ginsberg and Timothy Davies emphasize the "agony of decision-making" for education leaders making decisions affecting their coworkers. Ginsberg and Davies describe the personal toll paid as these leaders hid their emotions and displayed "the right corporate face" to appear confident and stable before their colleagues.[5]

To make matters worse, leaders are regularly bombarded with bad news about their policies, their programs, and the operation of their organization. I'm reminded of John Pittenger, an erudite and delightfully profane lawyer who was elected chief state school officer in Pennsylvania and found the job much more difficult than he expected. He tells the story of an assistant "who would come in each day with a long face and tell me about some new disaster. Finally, one day I exploded and said, 'Dammit, why don't you bring me some good news for a change? He rolled his eyes and walked out. About a week later he came in with a big smile and said, 'Guess what? The pigeons aren't shitting on the windowsills anymore,' and I said, 'Why are you telling me that?' He said, 'Well, you wanted some good news, and that's all I can think of.'"[6]

Of course, these difficult aspects of leadership are considerably increased when leaders promote significant change. These leaders will often be undercut, leadership mavens Ronald Heifetz and Marty Linsky argue, because people "want to be comfortable again, and you're in the way."[7] You might encounter personal attacks, marginalization, and efforts to divert you from your goals. You might also experience your own fear of losing your supporters' approval and affection.

Even if you're not knocked out of the game, education leaders work at the frontier of social change, where it is easy to make mistakes and where every move and utterance is scrutinized closely. Expectations are high, the margin for error slimmer every day. Indeed, it is likely that sometimes you will fall short of your hopes:

- You might fail in finding the right strategies to meet the high expectations of a key constituency group.
- You might make a public gaffe—a flip remark, a stupid mistake.
- You might be caught off guard and flummoxed as you struggle with unexpected events.
- You could be misunderstood—even vilified—and unable to respond because of confidential information.
- You might be rejected in your efforts to promote a new initiative.

Educators Richard Ackerman and Pat Maslin-Ostrowski contend that leaders are often "wounded," and that the resulting pain can feel "like a heart attack [and] reflects some of the same characteristics: loss of control, powerlessness, fear and vulnerability."[8]

In the wake of these realities, it is easy for many leaders to feel overwhelmed, misunderstood, fearful, disappointed, helpless, angry—and just plain awful. It is easy to feel unappreciated for your valiant efforts in defying the odds. In an environment where perfect pitch is expected and false notes amplified, the threat of feeling (and looking) like a fool is always lurking.

There are no two ways about it: leadership work can be really difficult. But the "harsh truth," Heifetz and Linsky remind us, "is that it is not possible to know the rewards and joys of leading without experiencing the pain as well."[9] And as my Harvard colleague Mary Grassa O'Neill also reminds us, we *can* rekindle the joy of being an education leader, "one of the hardest jobs you'll ever love."[10]

Making a
Hard Job Harder

It isn't the mountains ahead to climb
that wear you out; it's the pebble in
your shoe.

                              —Muhammad Ali

GIVEN THE ABUNDANT difficulties that mark the lives of many
education leaders today, it's important to ask how they handle
the stress. In this chapter, I examine how frazzled leaders experience discomfort and, in chapter 11, how they express it. Many
leaders muddle through by trying to fix their troubles in private and hide their troubles in public. And the consequences are
sobering: instead of dancing in the rain, many leaders make a
hard job a lot harder.

To understand how this unsettling pattern develops, take a
moment to imagine stumbling upon a patch of poison ivy, which
causes a rash that really itches. If you're like me, it's hard to resist
scratching the itch in an effort to fix the problem. If you do so,
however, you convert an unwelcome irritation into downright
suffering, which you have brought on yourself. A similar cycle

happens in leadership life. We encounter outside circumstances that trigger discomfort within us, and then we try to fix the problem. In doing so, we can magnify the pain and convert everyday discomfort into an even bigger problem.

Now, this idea may seem counterintuitive: that we—rather than our pressure-packed outside world—are the main cause of our woes. In what follows, I'll elaborate on this line of reasoning by describing how we typically react to discomfort and the high cost of doing so. But first let's briefly consider this puzzle: why are we so inclined to try to fix our internal discomfort?

THE FIXATION ON FIXING

Part of the reason we try to fix our discomfort is that we humans simply don't like to feel bad—and emotional upset feels awful. Indeed, many of us strive to escape disquieting situations because of our deep-seated desire to get back into our comfort zone and feel safe again. This desire has its roots in our evolutionary development, where escape from pain was essential for physical survival. We are uncomfortable with discomfort and take steps to get rid of it.

This proclivity to feel better is reinforced by societal expectations. Many of us have grown up learning that troubling feelings and thoughts are bad things that should be fixed or avoided. We have been taught to feel good and be happy—and think positive thoughts about others and ourselves. Particularly in Westernized societies, we have been taught that we should control our emotions and try to be nice.[1]

Psychologists Georg Eifert and John Forsyth remind us, for example, how "the little boy who cries on the playground is told, 'Pull yourself together; don't be a baby' . . . Through these and other experiences, children and adults learn to regulate their experiences and expression of their emotions . . . Emotional regulation is used as evidence of maturity, health and wellness, success, fulfillment, and happiness."[2] If we don't control our emotions, in short, we will fail to measure up to societal expectations.

Leaders try to control their upsets for reasons even deeper than the allure of their comfort zone and meeting societal expectations. Many leaders persist in seeing emotional discomfort as a daunting enemy because they believe that these negative feelings are a sign that they are weak—and thus not up to the job of being a leader. "The meaning of pain is failure to most of us," says my former organizational coach Barry Jentz.

Indeed, this propensity to fix our emotions is magnified for leaders because of widely accepted expectations of those in leadership positions. Leaders are supposed to be strong, tough, and decisive—to have the answers. They are supposed to be in charge. As leaders, we are supposed to control our work and our emotions. We are expected to be winners, not whiners.

FIXING DISCOMFORT

In leadership situations, we react to our problem of discomfort in many ways that can make a hard job harder. Most important, I believe, is excessive reliance on three reactions, which I call *self-defeating habits of the mind*. They are self-defeating in the sense that we get in our own way, inadvertently causing many of our own problems. They are habits because they happen automatically, that is, without careful thought. Rather than fixing our discomfort, these habits undermine effective leadership by triggering unskilled thoughts and actions that wear leaders down, as well as distract us from what we should be doing with our precious time.

In this chapter, I spotlight these three debilitating habits, which I call the three Rs:

- *resisting* the discomfort of leadership and trying to get rid of it
- *ruminating* excessively about flaws and failures and future foul-ups
- *rebuking* ourselves for not measuring up

To be sure, this description oversimplifies a complex set of reactions to discomfort, but my goal here is not to be comprehensive. Rather, I aim to provide busy leaders with a short list that is both memorable and manageable and that could make a big difference in their lives if they learned new ways to temper these three unhelpful habits.

Self-Defeating Habit 1: Resistance

To resist—withstand or oppose—is a good thing, especially when we are dealing with matters in the external world, such as unfairness or a jam at work. We take steps to fix the problem. What's more, resisting the way things are can provide internal relief in the short run. For example, if we need to concentrate on a high-stakes meeting, we can bury our troubling feelings for its duration, or take several deep breaths before such a meeting to temper our discomfort.

But what works temporarily in our external and internal worlds often backfires in the long run when it is applied to serious upsets. To resist our emotions, that is, to try to defeat them as if they were the enemy, is often a recipe for making things worse. As psychologists regularly remind us, *what we resist persists.*

This propensity to resist what's bugging us takes several overlapping forms, all aimed at dodging discomfort. A familiar approach is *suppression.* Uncomfortable thoughts and feelings are simply buried. Perhaps we don't allow ourselves to feel sad after firing a friend or to feel distraught after botching a decision. Many leaders fix the problem of discomfort, so the cliché goes, by sweeping negative thoughts and feelings under the rug.

A related way to resist—and "fix"— difficulties is to *escape* the problem causing them. Leaders might free themselves of anxiety by making a snap decision. They might get rid of their anger by withdrawing from a conflict situation. Or they could flee sadness through distraction.

A first cousin of escape is *avoidance*, and leaders learn a variety of methods to stay out of harm's way. Many leaders steer clear of the anxiety of change by becoming risk-averse. They distance themselves from the stress of interpersonal struggle by remaining aloof. Perhaps we duck a tough decision through procrastination. Indeed, psychologist Ron Siegel contends that avoidance is the number one cause of human misery.[3]

Over time, these common ways of resisting difficulties can morph into learned numbness. We might develop a thick skin to deaden biting criticism, or we replace optimism with cynicism. Worn down, a leader might learn to cope with the relentless pressure of work by becoming callous and emotionally comatose. And of course, there is always denial—we might simply refuse to admit to ourselves that we are feeling the pain of leading.

There are, without doubt, many leaders out there who do not engage in various forms of resistance. During my time as dean, however, I certainly did engage in these practices—and my guess is that this resisting behavior is a lot more prevalent than we would like to admit.

Self-Defeating Habit 2: Rumination

When faced with discomfort, many of us try to think our way out of it. Or when faced with a worrisome challenge, we go over and over it so that we are prepared. In common parlance, this inclination to ruminate is, of course, a really good thing. The problem is that we can overdo thinking—and easily get entangled in our thoughts and become their slave by believing that everything we imagine is true, even when our thoughts are harmful or disconnected from reality.

When everyday thinking morphs into a downward spiral of incessant, negative thoughts about the past and the future, psychologists see a big problem and call it rumination. "Ruminating is like a record that's stuck and keeps repeating the same lyrics," says psychologist Margarita Tartakovsky. This habit can lead to depression and anxiety—or just feeling beat and blue—and can distract us from doing what matters to us. Here are some common examples of rumination:

- brooding about feeling overwhelmed and out of gas
- stewing about the mess we'll be in if we don't get our act together
- rehashing a difficult conversation that pulled our chain
- asking the what-if question and then imagining catastrophic developments
- dwelling on what others think of us
- repeatedly picturing what we wish we had done
- obsessively rehearsing what we plan to say[4]

Education leaders, especially those who work at the K–12 level, can engage in still another form of rumination: doggedly reconsidering over and over again all the options in the hope that if enough information is collected, they'll find the very best approach for dealing with their most precious clients, children. There's a thin, hard-to-define line between productive thinking that produces a good decision and mind-numbing, repetitive thinking that gets us nowhere and leads to pessimism.[5]

Because our urge to eradicate our discomfort is greatly complicated by how our thinking minds work, let me elaborate. The core business of the wondrous human mind is the generation of thoughts. Each day, the average person generates an astounding seventeen thousand thoughts, at least according to one estimate.[6] That's more than a thousand thoughts each waking hour. At this rate, over a lifetime, the mind spews out millions of plans, judgments, memories, fantasies, and more. "Just as the salivary glands secrete saliva," says meditation teacher Jack Kornfield, "the mind secretes thoughts."[7]

To be sure, thought production can be pure joy. Academics, for example, just love to think—I know I do—and we are surrounded by scholars regularly lost in thought. A familiar Harvard story makes the point. As a preoccupied Professor Grozier (not his real name) enters an elevator, he asks a student, "Excuse me, in which direction was I walking?" She points to the left, and Grozier responds, "Ah, that means I did have lunch!"

What's more, leaders love to solve problems. It is exhilarating to diagnose causes, weigh alternatives, develop strategies, and encourage others to implement your seemingly brilliant ideas. This unique capacity of humans to think and to problem-solve is not only a joy, but also the key to the success of our species. This quality lets us subdue creatures that are stronger, faster, and far hardier than we are.

While thoughts can be extraordinarily helpful, they can also be surprisingly harmful, particularly when it comes to emotionally charged thoughts about internal discomfort. "Our mind's main job is to create thoughts," say psychologists Matthew McKay and Catherine Sutker. "That's what minds do—constantly, relentlessly. Some thoughts make sense; some don't. Some thoughts solve problems. Some paralyze us with fear. Some help us steer our ship. Some run us aground on the shoals of self-hate."[8]

It is not uncommon for leaders to become so closely identified with their troubling thoughts that they find it hard to disentangle themselves from their thinking, which they mistake for reality. For example, it's easy to imagine a leader feeling anxious about an action and jumping to the conclusion "I'm so bummed out by this stuff; I'm not fit for this job." Similarly, a leader making a gaffe in public might simply conclude, "I'm such a jerk."

When such mind chatter is taken as the truth, we can dwell on the past or worry too much about the future. Caught up in such thoughts, we might feel overwhelmed and become less effective. Under these circumstances, we often get in our own way of moving forward. But happily, we will be looking at learnable ways to head off unproductive rumination.

Self-Defeating Habit 3: Self-Rebuke

Remarkably, despite all that has been written debunking the idea that leaders should possess superhuman qualities, the myth of the solitary, heroic leader at the top often still holds sway in public discourse and in the minds of many leaders themselves. Given these expectations, it is not surprising that we see self-criticism as a way to keep ourselves on the ball and at our best at problem solving. And consequently, when things inevitably go awry, many of us lapse into self-rebuke and then conclude that we don't measure up as leaders.

Indeed, in my observations, self-rebuke runs rampant among leaders. Psychologist Christopher Germer says that when things fall apart, "more often than not, we feel ashamed and become self-critical: 'What's wrong with me?' 'Why can't I cope?' 'Why me?' Perhaps we go on a mission to fix ourselves, adding insult to injury. Sometimes we go after others. Rather than giving ourselves a break, we seem to find the path of greatest resistance."[9]

Here are some common examples of what self-rebuke looks like:

- harsh criticism for things we've said or done
- showing contempt for our personal flaws, our lack of perfection
- blaming ourselves for our failures without taking credit for any successes
- telling ourselves that we're lousy leaders[10]

In our hyperactive minds, many of us even create what I call the *measure-up monster*—MUM—that emerges from its cave waggling a censorious claw in our faces as we struggle to do a good job. In our darkest moments, MUM is always there voicing criticism and abuse: "You let that silly remark get to you? What a weakling!" "Leaders don't get confused—you're an impostor!" "What a wimp! Can't you make up your own mind?"

At the office, MUM has a ready response to every problem, telling us we have no business feeling discomfort, and thereby adds to our difficulties. So we allow MUM to dictate our actions, and we remain mum at the office. Try as we might to feel better, MUM makes us feel worse; we often feel helpless in its clutches.

The might of MUM no doubt differs among leaders. But given the superhuman expectations for leadership and the inevitability of falling short, it is hardly surprising that many of us see our discomfort as the enemy. After all, discomfort is not just a plain vanilla annoyance, but rather a harsh signal—and a reminder—that just maybe we are a flop as a leader. Added to our discomfort, then, is our dread of MUM leaving its cave and waving its poisonous talons. So we keep our MUM cornered in its cave by trying to control it—and burying our difficulties at the office.

Too Much of a Good Thing

Note that these three self-defeating habits of the mind exhibit a common property—all are too much of a good thing: too much resistance (when it comes to feelings), too much thinking, and too much self-criticism. Indeed, our weak points are our strong points taken to the extreme.

If we frame the three Rs in this way, the task ahead seems more manageable and less daunting. The goal is not to eliminate some basic flaws in your character, but rather to do a little less of what is often essentially a good thing to be doing in moderation. Indeed, if you can learn to just ratchet back your reliance on the three Rs, it can make a big difference in your leadership and life.

THE HIGH COST OF THE THREE Rs

For those of us who encounter difficulties at work and who beat ourselves up over them, it seems only natural to try to fix the problem. After all, problem solving is at the heart of what leaders do, and it certainly works in the physical world: if you are caught in a rainstorm, you put up your umbrella or skedaddle into a nearby shelter. Unfortunately, fixing problems doesn't work the same way in the psychological world, at least not in the long run. The more you try to get rid of your discomfort, the worse things can get—and the more you limit your potential to flourish as an effective leader.

Making Things Worse

One problem with the fixing approach is that internal upheavals can't be switched on and off like a light bulb. For better or worse, your fears and anxieties are very much a part of who you are as a human being. They burn brightest in your mind at times you cannot control—often sneaking up on you when you are least prepared to confront them. Meditation teacher Sylvia Boorstein puts it this way: "Even without preplanning, the top ten of our psychological-emotional hit parade have a way of marching into the mind whenever there is a break in the clouds. As soon as space allows, the mind ruminates over memories or reflects about the future—mostly with remorse or apprehension."[11]

And here's the big point: Not only can you not switch off your emotional discomfort, but recent research also shows that the struggle can turn ordinary pain into intense suffering. The more determined we are to fix our discomfort, the more the attempted solution becomes the problem. Steven Hayes, the father of acceptance and commitment therapy, contends: "The natural, rational thing to do when we face a problem is to figure out how to get rid of it and then actually get rid of it. In the external world, our ability to do just that is what allowed us to take over the planet. But that only works in the world outside the skin . . . [S]uffering is so pervasive because our attempts at solving it only make it persist."[12]

Another way to make the point: Trying to escape discomfort can be like trying to escape quicksand. The more you try to step out of it, the deeper you can sink into it. Counterintuitive as it might seem, the more you attempt to escape your discomfort, the more you can become trapped.

The core of the problem that Hayes and other psychologists are describing can be captured in a very rough rule of thumb about your inner life. Using the poison ivy metaphor, it goes like this:

Itching × Scratching = Self-Made Misery.

To take it another step, if we drop the metaphor and emphasize that the self-made misery is created by our minds, the rule of thumb becomes this:

Leadership Discomfort × Three Rs = Mind-Made Misery.[13]

This rule of thumb, of course, oversimplifies a complex set of concepts and processes and certainly doesn't fit every case. Nevertheless, it provides a useful way to capture the multiplicative role played by our habits of mind in causing the misery leaders often feel in dealing with their internal discomfort triggered by external pressures.

All in all, dissatisfied leaders are often those who want their internal life to be different from the way it is and who attempt to feel better—and less weak—by trying to fix their troubling reactions to reality. These leaders find it hard to resist solving the problem and, in doing so, can transform inevitable discomfort into avoidable mind-made misery.

Sidetracking Work

Struggling with your thoughts and emotions not only undermines your leadership, but can also hurt your organization, not to mention your health. For one thing, if you stay clear of situations that cause discomfort, it essentially means staying clear of leadership opportunities. After all, learning is at the heart of leadership, and learning produces (and sometimes requires) anxiety.

If you try too hard to avoid the stress of leadership, you might end up avoiding leadership altogether.

Moreover, dodging discomfort can be like holding down the lid on a boiling cauldron: the effort requires dedicated focus and energy and essential resources that could be better marshaled and deployed elsewhere; the only reward might just be a serious burn! In effect, choosing to control our discomfort means choosing to sidetrack our work and to hold ourselves back from doing what matters most to us—a high price to pay.

Attempts to control discomfort can also make us feel isolated. Comparing our insides with other people's outsides, we might start asking ourselves, "What's the matter with me? I shouldn't be in such pain. Other leaders aren't in this kind of turmoil." When we feel such sentiments often, we can unwittingly foster a conspiracy of silence. After all, we tell ourselves that it would be shameful to drop our mask and discuss how we truly feel. Moreover, constantly wearing a mask is like carrying a heavy weight. To always be on, particularly when you think you must prove that you measure up, can leave you exhausted and even feeling paralyzed. It takes courage to break this pattern.

Efforts to resist and fix can have additional negative organizational consequences:

- *Bad decisions:* If you take steps to get rid of complex problems quickly, you might be sacrificing the time and attention these issues deserve.
- *Undermined trust and credibility:* Your staff intuitively knows you are confused, furious, or mortified; not to acknowledge these feelings at all can make you appear out of touch.
- *Distance between you and your colleagues:* If your organization is under enormous stress, but you fail to acknowledge the personal costs, you might miss the chance to develop strong bonds of trust and norms of honesty, built on shared experiences.

And on top of all that, the stress of leadership can impair your health. In his fascinating book, *Why Zebras Don't Get Ulcers*, primatologist Robert Sapolsky argues: "Stress can wreak havoc with your metabolism, raise your blood pressure, burst your white blood cells, make you flatulent, ruin your sex life, and if that's not enough, possibly damage your brain. Why don't we throw in the towel right now?"[14] Well, we don't throw in the towel right now, because there is a workable alternative to what often feels like drowning in the rain.

Introducing
MY DANCE

CHAPTER THREE

The MY DANCE Framework

Life isn't about waiting for storms
to pass, but learning how to dance
in the rain.

—*Vivian Greene*

INSTEAD OF SEEKING shelter from the cloudbursts of stress and strain, consider an alternative approach that allows you to flourish in stormy weather—indeed, to dance in the rain. This approach constantly reminds you of your core values—what you stand for, the kind of person you want to be, the ideals that give your life meaning. With this framework, you build your capacity to handle the discomfort of leadership work and take care of yourself as you try to care for others. The familiar Serenity Prayer, attributed to theologian Reinhold Niebuhr, provides some guidance: "God, grant me the serenity to accept the things I cannot change, the courage to change the things I can, and the wisdom to know the difference."

THE SEVEN STEPS

We all would flourish more as leaders if we learned to accept our discomfort and focused our energies on actions that are consistent with our values—if we learned how to dance in the rain. The seven interconnected steps of MY DANCE evolved from my own struggles to achieve this balance. The framework of these steps aims to empower you to take advantage of your inner (and often hidden) strengths, to get beyond the upheavals of leadership, and to move toward a productive life of purpose, vitality, and joy. I offer no Pollyannaish promises here, but instead a way to make significant progress step by step.

MY DANCE builds on the belief, as noted earlier, that the main barrier to flourishing is not the discomfort caused by our upsetting experiences in the outside world, but rather the suffering caused by how we relate—and respond—to the discomfort inside our minds. I'm not talking here about something abstract or esoteric, but rather I'm suggesting concrete and less debilitating ways for our minds to process difficulties. Indeed, the seven steps are intended to deliberately disrupt unhelpful (yet typical) mental responses to difficulties, which regularly undermine our leadership. The steps are briefly summarized in the box "MY DANCE at a Glance"; we'll wade deeper into the complexities and subtleties of MY DANCE as we move ahead.

In introducing these steps, I'll mention a half dozen additional points that merit attention. First, while I've used MY DANCE as a way to help you remember the recommendations in this book, it is not the only way or necessarily the best way for you to map—and remember—this territory. Indeed, some educators feel awash in acronyms. If this is the case for you, then you might just explore the ideas presented on these pages and invent your own organizational stratagems.

Second, for convenience I've listed the seven steps as if each is distinct and equally important, with one step neatly following

MY DANCE at a Glance

M *ind your values*: Take action inspired by what matters most to you.

Y *ield to now*: Slow down and focus on the present moment.

D *isentangle from upsets*: Mentally step back, observing and making room for upsets.

A *llow unease*: Open up to upsets even if you dislike them.

N *ourish yourself*: Engage in activities that replenish your energy and restore your perspective.

C *herish self-compassion*: Give yourself the kindness you need and deserve.

E *xpress feelings wisely*: Carefully reveal your human side so that you can build trusting relationships.

another. In practice, of course, leadership life is messier. You may notice, for example, that the steps provide overlapping perspectives on the same complex terrain. You are encouraged to adapt and blend the different steps according to your own needs and circumstances rather than implementing them in a lock-step sequence.

Third, you'll notice there's no specific mention of mindfulness in the seven steps. Instead, I emphasize several of its component parts in the hope that this approach will facilitate your learning and memory.

Fourth, these steps grow out of my interest in the inner life of education leaders, the main audience for this book. I believe the demands of their work significantly amplify the stress of ordinary life, especially for leaders with direct responsibility for helping to shape the lives of children, teenagers, and young adults. But all these steps address universal issues facing human existence. So although I occasionally refer to education leaders, much of what I say applies to other kinds of leaders—and to everyone else.

Fifth, some people plain dislike dancing. They can feel left out because of physical limitations. Others feel self-conscious by being at the center of unwanted attention, which can lead them to compare their abilities with those of others. If this observation describes you, remember that dancing is used here as a metaphor for activities that make you come fully alive. If this metaphor doesn't work for you, you can substitute another activity that symbolizes bringing out your best.

Finally, these steps are a little like the training wheels on a bike; they're designed to provide some stability as you get rolling and deal with the ups and downs of falling off the bike by grounding you in an achievable number of things you can learn to do. As you become more skillful, you may find that you can discard these steps as you learn to ride this new bike in your own way.

At its core, MY DANCE offers a far-reaching and workable new way to view the connection between struggles with difficulties and flourishing (i.e., being in a vigorous state) as a leader. Surprisingly, you need not first feel good in order to flourish at work. You can simply have your difficult feelings and still live a vital life as a values-inspired leader. (Nevertheless, knowing how to implement these skills may certainly help you suffer less in the long run.)

The basic goal of MY DANCE, then, is not to get you back into your familiar but problematic comfort zone. MY DANCE is designed to move you toward flourishing and to enhance your effectiveness. It does this by changing the nature of your relationship with difficulties while nurturing your ability to keep a steady mind focused on wise actions, guided by the values that are most important to you.

THE ORIGINS OF *MY DANCE*

In developing the seven steps of MY DANCE, I've purposely dis-
tilled a lot of material into a limited number of steps and have
given this framework an easy-to-remember name. In doing so,
I've been inspired by Oliver Wendell Holmes, who once famously
said: "For the simplicity on this side of complexity, I wouldn't
give you a fig. But for the simplicity on the other side of complexity, for that I would give you anything I have."[1] The intention
is to keep the content as tight and focused as possible so that
it's easier to learn and easier to put unfamiliar perspectives into
practice, especially in difficult situations.

This framework is my own invention, but the ideas within
are borrowed from many specialists in different disciplines. Not
all readers are interested in the provenance of ideas—and this
may be especially true for education leaders loaded down with
unrelenting demands on their time. So, you may wish to jump
ahead to the chapters that guide you through learning the dance
steps. But if you are curious about how ideas evolve, the remain-
der of this chapter describes how my self-education in various
psychologies and contemplative practices culminated in the
writing of this book.

Teaching Courses on Leadership

My leadership experiences as dean of the Harvard Graduate
School of Education, described in chapter 1, shifted what I taught
and how I taught it. When I retired as dean in 2001 and returned
to the faculty, I changed my teaching focus from governmental
policy and qualitative methodology, my first loves, to leadership.
My aim was clear—to teach about leadership work as it truly is—
not what the textbooks said, not what society expected, not what
naive academics (like me) taught, but rather as it is when you are

living in a pressure cooker. I wanted to introduce a dose of reality into a field saturated with romantic notions of what leadership work entails.

Initially, my teaching spotlighted the outside work of leaders. I emphasized the big tasks of leaders—for example, creating strategy, mobilizing political support, building human capacity, overseeing operations, and handling crises. I also emphasized the unheroic side of leadership, the nitty-gritty of managing everyday vexing problems—those hard-to-define, devilishly complex issues with no solutions and whose best outcome is to identify the least bad option.

With this new teaching focus, I also stressed the importance of handling only those problems that belong on your plate. This approach is surprisingly complicated because employees typically view the boss as the problem solver. I've dubbed this attitude the *goose theory of leadership*. Honking and hissing like geese, faculty and staff members will cruise into the boss's office, ruffle their feathers, poop on the rug, and leave. This happened to me one summer morning, when a frantic staffer phoned me at home: "We've got a big dormitory problem. A new student says his room is filthy, with two used condoms under his bed!" Of course, this matter deserved prompt attention. But sensing that the problem was headed my way and believing that the on-site manager should take responsibility instead, I raised some questions and then closed with, "I know you can handle it."

Along the way, I also reminded my students that their job was not only to deal with problems but also to become troublemakers, that is, to make it difficult for those entrenched in old ways. (I once gave an opening address to new students urging them to become troublemakers; my student-services team was not pleased.)

As my teaching developed, my focus on the outside work of leaders was expanding to include teaching about the inside-the-skin complexities of leadership, how chiefs feel in the pressure cooker and how they handle upsets. As luck would have it, in

2005 my work was propelled in that direction by an invitation to write a chapter for a book about out-of-the box leadership.[2] Here was a chance to write about what had been percolating in my mind—ideas that I then called the pain of leadership. To get started on the chapter, I asked myself a simple question: "Who knows the most about pain?" After pondering the question for a while, I came up with two answers. Buddhists and shrinks, whose theories and practices I knew nothing about, were at the top of my list.

Moving Toward Mindfulness

As I was beginning to write my chapter on out-of-the-box leadership in the summer of 2006, I lucked out again. I was returning to Harvard from a visiting post at the University of Pennsylvania and was looking for a teaching fellow to assist me with my fall leadership course. By the time I got back to campus, all the students from the leadership wing of the Graduate School of Education were already committed to other courses. But then I noticed an application for the job from Metta McGarvey, an advanced doctoral student in the psychology department whose expertise was in adult development. Metta had experience working in nonprofits and in grassroots organizing, held two degrees in Buddhist studies, and was also a lifelong meditator as well. We hit it off right away. To make a long story short, we began teaching together, and we continue to do so until this day. Slowly but surely, a focus on the inner life of leaders and the practice of mindfulness became distinctive features of the course.

With a chapter to write and aided by Metta's wise counsel, I began to educate myself about pain and suffering and how to alleviate it—a process of self-education that continues to this day. In approaching my learning and writing, my data-gathering strategy has been to "soak and poke," a throwback to my earlier research on the politics of education and the down-to-earth jottings of political scientist Richard Fenno.[3] My soaking and poking looks like this: an informed colleague suggests a conference, which leads to several books to read, which leads to a retreat, which leads to a whole new line of inquiry, which leads to new teaching, and so on. Along the way, I've tried to put together, in a novel way, what I learned as I soaked and poked, puttering here and tinkering there as a bricoleur.

In my wanderings, I dug deep into Buddhism, not because of the allure of nirvana, but because it seemed as if its mind-training practices could be applied to leadership in a fairly secular way. I was also drawn to an optimistic view of human goodness and potential emanating from various teachers and contemplative texts. The Buddhism I was exposed to offered an intriguingly "light touch" when it comes to the human condition: it said, in my view, that all of us would be better off if we learned to just watch our hyperactive minds and not take our personal dramas quite so seriously.

I also dug deep into recent developments in modern American and European psychology, which increasingly is turning to ideas from Asian contemplative traditions for insights into dealing with the pain and suffering of life. I attended numerous workshops aimed at psychotherapists, not because I think leaders necessarily need therapy, but because the new mindfulness-based approaches might help high-functioning leaders. "The patterns of mind that keep people trapped in emotional suffering," psychologist John Teasdale and his colleagues remind us, "are fundamentally the same patterns of mind that stand between all of us and the flowering of our potential for a more deeply satisfying way of being."[4]

My understanding of mindfulness has been shaped by the groundbreaking work of scientists and clinicians much like Teasdale, who himself was one of the founders of mindfulness-based cognitive therapy.[5] Other exemplars include Susan Orsillo and

Lizabeth Roemer on anxiety relief; Marsha Linehan on dialectical behavior therapy; and, perhaps the best known of them all, Jon Kabat-Zinn on mindfulness-based stress reduction.[6]

In particular, I've been fascinated by acceptance and commitment therapy, the brainchild of Steven Hayes and several of his colleagues. This therapy encourages its practitioners to follow their values, accept whatever comes, and take their pain along for the ride. The therapy shines a bright light on going beyond stress reduction to becoming fully alive and leading a meaningful life, ideas appealing to those in leadership positions who are mission driven and want to make a difference in their lives. I've learned about all these programs through extensive reading and by attending numerous workshops and retreats, including a rewarding gathering aimed at leaders and led by Kabat-Zinn himself.

Much has changed in the few years since 2005, when I started my deep study of pain and suffering. Back then, few people I knew talked about meditation or contemplative practice at all. Now, however, it seems as if mental health professionals are clamoring to add mindfulness skills to their repertoire of interventions. A case in point: a September 2013 Harvard Medical School conference titled "Meditation and Psychotherapy" and featuring Zen master Thich Nhat Hanh sold out almost immediately and attracted more than twelve hundred mental health professionals.

This skyrocketing popular interest in meditation in part reflects preliminary scientific evidence that mindfulness-based approaches work. For example, Teasdale and colleagues sum up some benefits:

> One of the most exciting aspects of recent research has been the demonstration that mindfulness-based treatments can produce lasting beneficial changes in our brains. Mindfulness strengthens the brain's networks that regulate

emotional reactivity, reducing the size and impact of the amygdala—the fight, flight, or freeze system; it strengthens the networks that underlie our ability to feel compassion toward ourselves and others; and it changes the pathways that normally produce habitual and unhelpful brooding whenever sad mood arises.[7]

Indeed, the scientific community has been taking the concept of mindfulness quite seriously. For example, the October 2015 issue of *American Psychologist*, the official journal of the American Psychological Association, grapples with major topics in mindfulness research and practice.[8]

Moreover, the application of mindfulness to leadership is definitely on an upswing. Witness the 2013 World Economic Forum, held in Davos, Switzerland. "The hottest topic at this year's conference was mindfulness," says journalist Arianna Huffington. The stars at the conference "weren't the heads of state, foreign ministers, central bankers, billionaire investors or rock star activists," but rather the scholars and practitioners promoting the benefits of mindfulness. "If Davos is the center, I think it's now safe to say mindfulness has come in from the fringes."[9]

Almost overnight, the practice of mindfulness in the modern world has moved from widespread skepticism and obscurity to ubiquity. Indeed, it's amazing to witness its increased adoption in fields ranging from medicine to education to sports to the workplace. As an academic, of course, I am a bit cautious: the scientific community is still in the early stages of documenting how mindfulness works. Despite much promising research so far, there's always a risk that this ancient practice will be oversold as a proven elixir for all that ails us. These cautions notwithstanding, I believe today's exploding interest in mindfulness is a wonderful step forward, with significant potential for leaders. The practice is worth pursing with vigor, rigor, and enthusiasm.

Other Approaches

Beyond mindfulness, my thinking has also been shaped in important ways by the innovative work of Christopher Germer, Kristin Neff, and their colleagues on self-compassion, which is intimately related to mindfulness. Their well-deserved fame has skyrocketed over the past few years, and step 6 of MY DANCE is all about self-compassion (see chapter 10). Also newly prominent in the field of psychology is the focus on positive psychology—and in chapter 9, "Nourish Yourself," I devote attention to Rick Hanson's work, which is grounded in a combination of positive psychology, brain science, and contemplative training.

In addition to these powerful approaches, two others—focusing and internal family systems (IFS)—have influenced my thinking and have led to several exercises in the book. These two approaches differ somewhat from mindfulness on the nature of our upsets, on what lies at our core, and on how to be with our inner rumblings. For the purposes of this book, you need not be acquainted with the details of focusing and IFS, but do read through the endnote if you want to learn more.[10]

As an outside observer of psychology, I look forward to the grand synthesis of these five complementary approaches to enhancing well-being—mindfulness, self-compassion, positive psychology, focusing, and IFS. In the meantime, in the pages ahead, I make a first attempt at integrating elements of these approaches, with a particular focus on education leaders.

A Workshop Is Born

As I learned more about the inner dimensions of leading, and as Metta and I grew more confident in our teaching, we decided to pool our knowledge and seek approval to cochair a new Harvard workshop, called the Inner Strengths of Successful Leaders.[11] These four-day workshops are aimed at current education leaders across the K–12 and college levels from all over the United States and abroad. The workshop kicked off in 2011, with the following course description:

> During this experiential program, you will work with scientifically based mindfulness practices. Guided by faculty with decades of mindfulness and leadership experience, you will learn to deepen your presence, wisdom, focus and ability to stay calm and centered. You will learn how to better manage uncomfortable feelings and difficult interactions, think more clearly and compassionately, discern where to direct your time and energy, sustain your enthusiasm, and achieve results. These essential inner strengths will help you to take stress in stride, make wise decisions, and savor the joy of leadership.

We've been humbled by participants' enthusiasm for the workshop. "This is the most profound experience I have had in my twenty-five years of teaching," one school superintendent said in a fairly representative comment.

The workshop has allowed Metta to adapt her deep understanding of the emotional development of adults, Buddhism, and the teaching of mindfulness to the real lives of busy leaders. And the program has allowed me to develop, try out, and revise my slowly emerging framework, MY DANCE, the focus of this book.

Through the workshops, we have been able to collect some preliminary numbers on the stress experienced by educators in the field. (Incidentally, in developing the workshop, we were struck by the absence of systematic, longitudinal research on the stress of education leadership.) To gather data, we have administered, at the beginning of several workshops, an informal survey that asks about the "human side of leading." Each year, the results have been remarkably consistent and revealing. Let's look at 2013, for example (the numbers in parentheses show the percentages of participants who answered "almost always," "often," and "sometimes," respectively):

- A total of 98 percent felt overwhelmed by all the "stuff" on their plates (16, 55, 27).
- A total of 93 percent expressed doubts about their ability to lead (7, 45, 41).

In the face of these difficulties:

- A total of 86 percent reported bouts of stewing (24, 33, 29).
- A total of 88 percent took steps to get rid of their discomfort (22, 38, 28).
- A total of 90 percent rebuked themselves for performing imperfectly (34, 29, 27).
- A total of 96 percent neglected self-care in the midst of stress (26, 39, 31).

To be sure, abundant care needs to be taken in drawing conclusions from our informal surveys, particularly when the respondents are attending a workshop focused on the difficulties of leadership. Nonetheless, I've been struck by the large numbers of participants willing to acknowledge these problems, which in our culture are often viewed as signs of being weak.

Reality at Home

Not all my luck has been good. This book reflects not only my work experiences, but also a recent life-shattering event in my family. On November 20, 2012, my wife Susan was diagnosed with Alzheimer's disease. I will share more of this experience with you in the detailed description of Step 6, self-compassion, in chapter 10. For now, suffice it to say that I'm trying to learn each day from this unwanted experience and use the lessons learned about handling upsets to hone the seven steps of MY DANCE, which now also serves as my guide and lifeline as a caregiver.

Getting Ready to Dance

Then my father sat down beside him, put his arm around my brother's shoulder and said, "Bird by bird, buddy. Just take it bird by bird."

—*Anne Lamott*

IN THE NEXT seven chapters, I dig deep into the seven steps of MY DANCE, one step at a time. But first, in this short chapter, I want to emphasize the importance of practice in learning the steps—and suggest how you might approach this part of the book.

THE EXERCISES AHEAD

Sprinkled throughout the discussions of the steps, you'll find around three dozen exercises that, taken together, aim at developing both knowledge about the seven steps of MY DANCE and the know-how required for putting these steps into action (see the appendix for a summary of these exercises). Learning these steps is a little like learning to swim. You can read about swimming and talk about swimming, but reading and talking will only take you so far. You need to jump into the pool, experience what it's like, and practice the strokes.

The exercises presented here include guided meditations, experiential activities, and self-analyses that help you to focus on *experience* (either real or imagined) and to go beyond just reading the book. As you work through these exercises, you will rely on your imagination and powers of observation—and sense of humor—to gain a visceral sense of the material. The exercises complement the poems, song lyrics, and personal stories scattered throughout the book. Taken together, all this material is meant to enhance your understanding and build the skills at the heart of MY DANCE.

Throughout my discussion of the seven steps, I include several short-pause exercises that can help busy leaders settle down and open a mental space for wise choices and considered action. "Between stimulus and response there is a space," says Viktor Frankl. "In that space is our power to choose our response. In our response lies our growth and our freedom."[1]

Before you jump in, keep in mind a few additional points about the exercises:

- What I'm offering is a sampler of activities to try, certainly not a comprehensive list; indeed, you are invited to invent your own exercises.
- Some exercises require repeated practice to build your know-how, while others need only to be tried once or twice to enhance your understanding.
- As noted earlier, MY DANCE addresses matters facing all human beings, not just leaders in education. Similarly, the best exercises, many of which originate outside the field of education, also have a broad scope. Wherever it's helpful, I've linked generic exercises more closely to the lives of education leaders.

- Several exercises come from workshops I've taught and attended—group exercises that I believe lend themselves to easy adaptation for your own individual practice.
- Some exercises suggest written reflection at the end of the activity; you might want to invest in a journal.
- Each exercise is carefully set off in the text so that it's easy to locate, and the instructions are clearly marked.

Taken together, the exercises offer sufficient variety that I'm bound to offend everyone, as my Harvard colleague Bob Kegan is gleefully wont to say. If you find yourself shaking your head over a particular exercise or suggestion, you might think of your reaction as an unexpected "growth opportunity," so to speak, to practice how to handle perturbations.

As you read the book for the first time, I hope you'll give all the suggested activities at least passing attention to see if they may be helpful. In the longer run, I invite you to pick and choose among the multiple exercises and use those that work for you as you further refine your skills.

PREPARING FOR PRACTICE

In preparing to engage with the suggested activities, you might find it helpful to spend a moment or two getting ready and comfortable, both physically and mentally. Preparation is particularly important when you repeatedly practice various formal meditations—and not surprisingly, different meditation teachers emphasize different details, which are spelled out in numerous books and recordings.

In my view, the essence of getting ready entails finding a quiet place, if you can, where you can slow down from the rush of life and not be interrupted; positioning your body so that you're comfortable, relaxed, alert, and grounded in the earth; and inclining your mind toward developing in-the-moment awareness of your thoughts, feelings, body sensations, and external surroundings. Depending on the circumstances and the exercise, you can practice while sitting (either on a chair or a cushion), lying down, or even standing up or walking. Indeed, you can practice meditating while waiting in a noisy line, sitting at an airport gate, or standing in an elevator. As appropriate, you can close your eyes or keep them open with a soft gaze on a spot in front of you. (In presenting the exercises on the pages that follow, I've assumed that preparing for practice is implicit in the instructions. Therefore, I won't repeat the preparatory steps presented in this section, but feel free to flip back to this section anytime for a refresher.)

Preparation is important, and so too is setting aside time for regular practice and contemplation. Not surprisingly, there's no consensus on how much time is both practical and ideal. In my view, regularity is more important than duration. It's much more useful to set aside dedicated time—even just a few minutes every day at the same time and in the same place—than it is to aim for long but irregular periods. In my case, I aim for at least fifteen minutes every day when I get up; most days—but not all—I follow through with this goal. You need to decide what works for you and aim to build the daily habit.

In choosing how to spend your practice time, you might start with a rough assessment of your needs. You probably already have some intuition about which steps need a little extra attention. (See chapter 11 for a more detailed discussion of self-assessment and for my "fiddler crab test," which may help you discover the areas you'd like to work on.)

Tailored to each step, these various exercises can be combined into daily mental workouts, which are a little like the multiple exercises you do at the gym to develop your different muscle groups. Mental workouts can help build both the knowledge and the know-how—the mental muscles, if you will—necessary for understanding and implementing the seven steps of MY DANCE.

Like any set of muscles, they will grow with proper repetition; without repeated attention and practice, they will atrophy.

SAVORING CAMPBELL'S SOUP

As you approach this part of the book, I invite you to think of it as you would a can of Campbell's chicken noodle soup. It is highly condensed, and additional ingredients are needed to make it appetizing and digestible.

One key ingredient is gentleness toward yourself. This ingredient is important, because I'm asking you to dig deep, see things as they really are, and address personally sensitive issues, and this intense scrutiny can be scary. A second vital ingredient is time and space. If you speed-read through the seven steps in one sitting, checking them off your to-do list, you might miss the subtleties of how MY DANCE may be helpful to you. I suggest that you read, ponder, experience, and savor the seven steps at an unruffled pace, perhaps focusing on one step at a time with sufficient pauses in between to allow yourself to absorb the material in your mind, your heart, and your body.

PART III

MY DANCE,
Step by Step

Mind Your Values

Life is never made unbearable by circumstances, but only by lack of meaning and purpose.

—Viktor E. Frankl

In a Nutshell ...

What This Step Is

- The ability to identify your core values—*what matters most* to you
- The willingness to *take action* inspired by these values, even when it hurts

What This Step Helps You Do

- Clarify, remember, and act on your values, which can infuse your leadership with a sense of meaning, purpose, and vitality
- Develop the motivation, commitment, and willingness to do what matters most to you, even when you want to escape an uncomfortable situation
- Lead a life shaped by your values, instead of one ruled by emotions, the minutiae of life, or the wants of others

M

Y

D

A

N

C

E

APPLES AND TREES

When I was growing up, my father was obsessed with protecting his family from danger. He worried most about fires, burglaries, and germs—and took inventive protective action, often to the bemused looks of his children. To guard against a house break-in, for example, he decided to make our back-porch door burglar-proof. With a heavy rubber band, he attached the skeleton key to the door handle so that a thief couldn't slide a piece of paper under the door, dislodge the key with a pencil pushed through the keyhole, and then fetch the key by withdrawing the paper. Believe me, our house was the safest on the street.

According to family lore, my dad grew up believing that life was either dangerous or a sin. Perhaps he felt that way because he was raised in a rather strict, devout family in rural Kentucky at a time when Irish Catholics faced serious discrimination. For whatever reasons, my dad turned out to be an innovative educator, a gentle soul devoted to his family—and also an anxious man, a master of worst-case analyses. He didn't originate Murphy's Law, but he sure lived it.

This apple in some ways didn't fall far from the family tree. I slid through high school, but my anxiety went through the roof while I was an undergraduate at Columbia University, a very competitive place filled with highly verbal students always eager to win an argument. For whatever reasons, my anxiety crystalized around a dread of being called on in class. I was fearful of not measuring up and looking like a fool. As a result, I searched for courses requiring little student participation, eschewing those that might be of more interest. Looking back, I now realize that I organized much of my college life around avoiding danger, dodging classes where I was likely to be put on the spot. Like Houdini, I became an accomplished escape artist.

I tell this story because I believe things might have been different had I followed the step explored in this chapter. Back then, I rarely thought about my personal values—about what was really important to me. I was unaware of the ways my life was being jerked around by my fears—and blind to the sacrifices I was making. It never occurred to me that I could learn to identify my core values, act on them, and, at the same time, learn to take my anxiety along for the ride.

M

LEADING WITH YOUR VALUES

Flourishing means living a life inspired by your core values—the opposite of what I did in college. It means leading with the values you care most about. Drawing on the pioneering work of psychologist Steven Hayes and his colleagues, I call this kind of behavior *values-inspired action* (VIA).[1] VIA is critical in creating a life marked by meaning, purpose, and vitality and in turn is critical to your long-term effectiveness as a leader. Because of VIA's importance, you can begin the seven steps of MY DANCE by exploring what really matters to you and by translating your values into action, even when it hurts.

To start, you might ask yourself what currently motivates your leadership. Might it be a desire to feel comfortable—by avoiding stress, steering clear of painful emotions, doing the bidding of others, or playing it safe—indeed, acting like Houdini? Might it be a need to feel less overwhelmed, by slogging through the endless—and often mind-numbing—items on your to-do list? Or might you be motivated by what matters most to you, even when it makes you feel anxious or uncomfortable? The truth is that being preoccupied with comfort and self-protection can undermine your sense of purpose and meaning. The preoccupation can undermine a key element of leadership—namely, taking actions that reflect your very own core values.

This trade-off between values and comfort is captured in a story that I once saw on a poster in an administrator's office:

Joe had the finest lamb in all of Armenia, with the longest and softest fleece. The lamb was so famous that Joe's neighbors decided to steal it. When he saw them coming, Joe carried the lamb into his cabin, barred the door, and began racing from window to window, shooting at the robbers. But each time Joe crossed the room, he tripped and fell over the frightened lamb. In frustration, he opened the door and kicked the lamb out of the house, so he could continue shooting.

In our efforts to remain safe in our comfort zone, many of us, like Joe, lose sight of what's important to us, and without thinking, we kick our values out the door. In the heat of the moment, we forget the importance of meaning in our lives, as articulated by Viktor Frankl in his best-selling book, *Man's Search for Meaning*, published some seventy years ago, about his experiences at Auschwitz.[2] Carolyn Gregoire of the *Huffington Post* succinctly summarizes Frankl's influential view that "meaning, not success or happiness, is the driving pursuit of human life."[3]

Indeed, your values can motivate you to take action that keeps you on the path to what really matters to you, even when you are stressed, confused, or overwhelmed. Your values are the very soul of who you are and the kind of life you want to live as a leader and a person. Leadership guru Ron Heifetz and his colleagues make the point this way: "It makes little sense to practice leadership and put your own professional success and material gain at risk unless it is on behalf of some larger purpose that you find compelling . . . Clarifying the values that orient your life and work and identifying larger purposes to which you might commit are courageous acts. You have to choose among competing, legitimate purposes, sacrificing many in the service of a few. In doing so, you make a statement about what you are willing to die for, and therefore, what you are willing to live for."[4] In a word, your values lie at the heart of flourishing as a leader.

In this view, it is crucial to reflect deeply on your core values and keep them front and center in your consciousness. Your values include what you treasure and stand for; your deepest aspirations for the kind of person you want to be; the qualities you want to display as a human being; how you want to treat others; and even your heartfelt yearnings for how you wish to be remembered.

In doing this reflection, you might confuse goals with values, but the two are very different. Goals may be some distant point ahead—for example, the timely completion of an excellent report, the implementation of a new program, or the development of staff skills. But, like the stars overhead, values are always with us, helping us chart our course. For example, we might be pursuing social justice, promoting trust and honesty, or trying to be a kind person. Goals are achievable outcomes in the service of our values. Goals speak to our destinations; values speak to our journey.

The essence of values is captured in the first line of a popular song that Dionne Warwick sang so beautifully in the 1960s: "What's it all about, Alfie?" You might ask yourself, "What will bring me a sense of purpose? What will speak to my search for meaning? What do I want my leadership life to be all about?"

In what follows, you will learn how to clarify your values and put them into action. This chapter includes a focus on the obstacles to this step. In the spirit of a primer, I aim to present the essentials, leaving it to others to address all the nuances, such as the sometimes-tricky task of dealing with conflicting values.[5]

CLARIFYING YOUR VALUES

Many of you, like me, probably haven't spent a lot of time slowing down, stepping back, and thinking about what really matters to you. We've been preoccupied with the rat-a-tat of our busy lives and the joys and sorrows that leadership and life regularly bring. So, we will begin with several exercises that might help you clarify your values.

The exercises in this chapter are all designed to help you pause and reflect—and begin to identify the values that mean the most to you as a leader. You can do this first exercise, "Favorite Leader," by yourself, but it also works well in groups, where you can share comments at the end of the activity.

FAVORITE LEADER *(10–15 minutes)*

Begin by recalling from your life someone who is engaged in leadership and whom you have particularly admired. The person could be a school principal, a teacher, a counselor, a college administrator, or someone else, perhaps outside the field of education. The leader could be a former boss, a colleague, or someone you admire from afar. If the person is close to you, try to choose someone with whom you've had a mostly positive relationship. For now, it's best to avoid choosing someone who elicits complicated or confusing emotions. Take a couple of minutes to identify your favorite leader.

Next, reflect for several minutes on this person's values— that is, what this leader stands for, the qualities displayed as a human being, how he or she behaves and treats others.

Now, reflect for several minutes on how this individual makes you feel. Fully savor in your body the warmth and joy of your recollections.

As this short exercise comes to an end, take a moment to silently express your gratitude for what this person means to you.

When you are ready, open your eyes, and if you can, take a moment to write out your reflections on a sheet of paper or in your journal. If you are part of a group, share your perspectives on your favorite leader's values and on how the person makes you feel before penning your reflections.

M

When I think of the foregoing activity, my mind immediately turns to Nelson Mandela. I had the good fortune to work in the townships of South Africa on an education reform project in the early 1990s just as apartheid was ending and as Mandela was getting out of jail. Like so many others, I was inspired by his bravery, his steadfastness, and his remarkable lack of bitterness. But what I remember most came years later, in 1998, when Mandela received an honorary degree at Harvard at a special event for him. At the end of the ceremony, surrounded by security guards eager to whisk him off the stage, Mandela paused and asked the Kumba Singers, a group of black undergraduates who had performed before him, to come forward. One by one, he unhurriedly shook their hands and said thank you, leaving not a dry eye among them. When I need inspiration—and I often do—I think of this powerful world figure with an iron will but who was also disarmingly kind and gentle.

In addition to looking outward to admired leaders to help clarify your values, it's also helpful to look at your own inner life. One good way to do so is to contemplate the time when you will retire and reflect back on your life. The following exercise, "Retirement Party," will help you do just that.

RETIREMENT PARTY   *(15–20 minutes)*

Imagine being at your retirement party. The time has come to interrupt the festivities so that people can share their prepared remarks about you. Think about what you would most want your colleagues, family, and friends to say about you—about the kind of education leader you are, the kind of life you lead, the values you've held dear during your career. In particular, imagine the speakers addressing these four dimensions of your work:

- *Relationships:* what matters most to you in your interactions with colleagues and others. You might want to hear, for example, that you always had time to listen to every teacher's concerns.
- *Tasks:* what you aimed for in getting the work done. For example, perhaps people will speak about your devotion to excellence and equity in serving students, especially those who came from the poorest families.
- *Process:* what matters to you in how a job gets done and who needs to be involved. Perhaps you will hear about your focus on inclusion, collaboration, and respect for divergent views.
- *Work–life balance:* what you hope for in making time for both your job and the rest of your life. You might want to hear, for example, about your commitment to making quality time for your family, friends, and community—and your commitment to enabling your colleagues to do so as well.

When you are ready, open your eyes if they had been closed. Then, write down what you would most like to hear. When you are done, take a moment, and then slowly read to yourself what you have written, savoring every word.

A variant on the above activity is for you to visualize your own funeral many years ahead. I've often used both the preceding exercise and the following one when working with leaders. It goes like this: Imagine being seated in a corner where you can see and hear everything, but nobody can see you. What would you most want people to say? Write down what you hope to hear. To top things off, also imagine the headstone on your grave, and write out the epitaph that captures the essence of your life. In doing this somber exercise, you might add a little levity by remembering comedian George Carlin's lighthearted words: "Life's journey is not to arrive at the grave safely, in a well

M

preserved body, but rather to skid in sideways, totally worn out, shouting 'holy shit . . . what a ride.'"[6]

These exercises above ask you to recall what matters to you. For many of us, however, it's easier to recognize our values when we are confronted with them explicitly than it is to recall them out of thin air. So here's an exercise that lists three dozen words that point to values commonly found among education leaders. Of course, there's nothing magic about the following list. I am not trying to be comprehensive or suggest that there are certain right answers. But through these exercises, you can begin to decide what's important to you, to think about your top values as a leader and a person.

In the following exercise, "Seven Top Values," you'll be asked to identify several key values.[7] You might never have thought much about identifying these values, so give yourself time to slow down and reflect.

SEVEN TOP VALUES   (20–30 minutes)

Please read through the entire exercise and carefully examine, one by one, the list of common values below to get a sense of what's coming. In going through the list, note that the values fall into two overlapping categories: the first three columns speak to the *kind of person you want to be* in your interactions with others; the fourth column speaks to *what you stand for in life*.

Don't forget to add at the bottom of the list any additional values that may have surfaced from the preceding exercises or that otherwise come to mind.

Now go through the list, and circle each value that's very important to you. If this is difficult, don't worry. While some values are easy to identify, others may well lie below the surface of your normal thinking.

Taking your time, go through all your circled values and select seven that matter the most to you, marking each one with a star. If you are unsure, that's neither a problem nor unusual. Indeed, some of our values, and the intensity with which we hold them, are often discovered in the process of taking specific action. So, just do the best you can to get an approximate list.

Altruistic	Effective	Humorous	Diversity
Authentic	Empathic	Innovative	Equity
Aware	Fair	Kind	Excellence
Caring	Family focused	Loving	Hard work
Collaborative	Friendly	Responsible	Integrity
Compassionate	Generous	Tolerant	Justice
Courageous	Grateful	Transparent	Lifelong learning
Curious	Healthy	Trustworthy	Service
Diligent	Humble	Wise	Showing up

With your list in hand, now take several minutes to write a sentence or two explaining why each of the seven values you've starred is particularly important to you. Later, when you have the time, you may want to put your list of seven on index cards to be used as a handy reference. I carry my index cards in a special bag in my backpack. I also have a list of my top values on an app on my smartphone. Symbolically (and physically!), my values travel with me wherever I go.[8]

Taking time to clarify our personal values is central to leadership work. Indeed, as my colleague Robert Peterkin is wont to say, "If you don't stand for something, you'll sit still for anything." And yet our values are easily forgotten or are never made explicit in the first place, as we saw earlier in the story of my risk-avoiding college experience and in the tale of Joe and the lamb. But it need not be this way. This lesson was driven home for me during a recent experience involving, of all things, a lost hat. If our values are uppermost in our minds, I learned, they can have a big influence on our behavior, even in the rush of life. Here's the hat story.

While working on this chapter, I found myself reflecting deeply about my values and the ways they affect my life. I realized that a value that means a lot to me is kindness, which comes from observing my mother. In all honesty, I also began to realize that my values are often among the last things on my mind, what with the pressures of daily life.

While contemplating these matters of values, I was asked to attend a meeting in downtown Boston, about thirty minutes away from my office by subway. It turned out that the meeting was unproductive, failing to deliver what I expected. As I left, I felt grumpy for wasting so much time.

As I headed back to the subway, I observed an elderly man lose his hat, which got swept across two lanes of heavy traffic by a howling wind. He stopped for a moment, looked at the speeding cars, and walked on. There I was, ambling along, feeling sorry for myself, rehashing what had happened at my annoying meeting, when my mind shifted to my recent preoccupation with values and my focus on kindness. I began to wonder whether this gentleman might have lost a treasured possession. I stopped walking, surveyed the situation, crossed the road with care, and picked up his hat, which was now wedged against a curb.

By the time I got back to his side of the street, the man was gone. I then spotted him two blocks ahead and began to run. I called out to him while waving his hat. He looked confused as I approached at a trot. His surprised look turned into a huge smile when I handed him his hat. I smiled back and wished him well as he continued on his way.

Ten minutes later, I got back to the subway stop, hoping I had brought some unexpected joy to this elderly gentleman—and knowing that the experience had brought meaning and joy to my day. It lifted my mood and shifted my attention from rehashing a bad meeting to being fully present in the moment.

I silently thanked my mother for helping me remember to do what matters.

PUTTING VALUES INTO ACTION

In MY DANCE, knowing what matters is crucial, but it's not enough. The aim is *to enable you to change your behavior*, and this not only requires that you remember your values, but also that you understand what concrete actions will move you toward your values. Values-inspired action requires strategies for dealing with the major obstacles to taking such action, obstacles that not only can sidetrack your attention but also can undermine your best efforts to take VIA.

These obstacles come in basically three flavors. First are emotional blocks to action, such as fear of failure, disapproval, depression, anxiety, shame—or an especially big bugaboo for leaders, fear of looking weak. Second are mental obstacles caused by the tendency of our hyperactive minds to judge, compare, and spew out unhelpful thoughts. And third are more practical problems caused by a lack of information and the absence of problem-solving skills. As discussed earlier in this book, these obstacles often show up in life as the three Rs: *resistance* to our troubling emotions, a surefire recipe for complicating our lives; *rumination* as we obsess over the past and the future; and *rebuking* ourselves for not measuring up.

To be sure, facing these obstacles in the pursuit of VIA can be quite costly. But as psychologist Matthew McKay and his colleagues remind us, "If we don't face these demons, we end up doing nothing. Each opportunity to pursue what matters slips away, making living a valued life even more elusive."[9]

All these obstacles—and their personal costs—are addressed in later chapters. We'll learn how to handle our negative emotions, calm our peripatetic minds, and take them a lot less seriously. We'll also learn how to detect when we are about to react impulsively and how to deliberately disrupt the three Rs before they take over our lives. The goal is not to eliminate these obstacles, which is usually a recipe for making things worse, but rather to relate to them in a different way. This reduces their debilitating power over us and helps clear the way for VIA.

Because pain, like gravity, will always be with us, VIA also requires a strong sense of commitment. Indeed, committed action entails being bound, emotionally and intellectually, to behaving in a way that serves your values. It implies a readiness and the courage to fully experience the pitfalls of leading, a willingness to face the cost of a valued action and go ahead anyhow, and the grit to persevere when swamped by the storms of leadership.

The notion of committed action is captured for me in a verse from Ecclesiastes: "Whatever thy hand findeth to do, do it with all thy might." In the end, it is this commitment—and willingness to do what it takes—that allow us to remain true to our deepest values when everything in us is screaming to run for the cover of our comfort zone.

This discussion of VIA has particular relevance to those many leadership situations where you need to make a split-second decision after a painful stimulus. You can make a decision in accordance with what really matters to you, or you can choose to make yourself feel better in the moment, as I did in selecting courses when I was in college. Comparing these alternatives sharpens the question that you need to ask as an education leader in these trying moments: "How can I remain true to my core values, and willingly pay the price, rather than focusing on escaping my discomfort?"

Well, all that's a mouthful to digest, so here's another activity, which I hope will help illuminate the main points so far—and help you put them into action. Building on the preceding "Seven Top Values" exercise, the next exercise, a follow-up, aims to help you

M

- better understand what's meant by VIA;
- develop a deeper appreciation of VIA's importance in your work and life;
- make VIA central in your work, even when it pushes you outside your comfort zone; and
- get specific, by generating six concrete steps that you can implement immediately.

I call this learning tool "Viva VIA!" because I hope "Long live values-inspired action!" becomes your rallying cry as a leader.

VIVA VIA! *(20–30 minutes)*

1. Read through the entire exercise so you have a sense of what's coming.

2. Drawing from your list of seven top values in the last exercise, choose three values for priority attention in this exercise. Pick three values for which you can envision action steps that will move you toward your values. For example, you might choose "collaborative" from your list of seven because you know what action is needed to include parents who are currently excluded from school policy making. (The reason for choosing just three values is to keep this exercise manageable. Feel free to include more.)

3. Write out on a piece of paper your three priority values, leaving space under each for two proposed action steps, to be added later, for a grand total of six action steps.

4. Under each of your three priority values, identify one action step that you feel comfortable about implementing. For example, if one of your priority values is being more family focused, a proposed action step might be something like this: "Starting next Monday, I'll set aside three specific nights each week for family dinners." In thinking about your actions, remember to keep them doable and as specific as possible.

M

5. Turning to the hardest part of VIA—taking action inspired by your values, even when it hurts—identify one additional action step for each priority value, steps likely to make you feel uncomfortable. For example, if you value being a visible leader, you might commit to a schedule of high-profile speeches, even though public speaking makes you anxious. If you value social justice, you might commit to aggressive tactics with opponents of extra help for poor children, even though you are allergic to conflict. Or, if you put a high premium on being innovative, you might pursue a high-risk project focused on increasing student participation in governance, even though you abhor the likely controversy. Write out this more difficult action step under each priority value. Again, remember to keep the steps doable and as specific as possible.

6. When you are finished recording your six action steps— two for each priority value—take a moment to visualize both putting these actions into place and how you would feel. On the flip side of the paper, record what comes to mind. Finally, reflect in writing, perhaps in your journal, on what you have learned from this exercise.

This exercise spotlights the reality that taking action inspired by your values can be really difficult. An often-cited exemplar is Charles Darwin, who spent five years on HMS *Beagle*, guided by his commitment to the advancement of natural science, even though ocean travel made him violently seasick. Another exemplar is the great British actor Laurence Olivier, who was willing to step out on stage even though he suffered from debilitating bouts of stage fright. Instead of running for cover, both men squarely faced the high costs of doing what they valued and were willing to do it anyway, taking their discomfort with them.

The "Viva VIA!" exercise also reminds us that leaders regularly promote change—and we all know that change can be painful. The idea is to follow your dreams as a leader, investing your time in doing what really matters, and work with your discomfort skillfully, rather than trying to get rid of it. Then, and perhaps only then, can you effectively choose your direction and begin to change the external things that can be changed.

This, of course, is easier said than done. It takes courage to change. Indeed, it takes courage for leaders to seek out what I call the *leadership zone*—the boundary between what we know and what we don't know—the place where we do the necessary work of learning new ways. For many leaders, being in this zone is often accompanied by feelings of anxiety and confusion. We need courage to work on this frontier, with all the doubts and fears of getting lost. We must hold steady—and show equanimity—in the midst of the unsettling uncertainty and conflict that marks organizational change. In short, we need personal strength to fully embrace change and all the difficulties it entails.

In sum, I invite you to clarify—and remember—your core values, take action inspired by them, choose to change what you can, muster the courage to do it, and willingly take your discomfort along on your leadership adventure. In doing so, I also invite you to remember the wise words of Friedrich Nietzsche: "He who has a why to live can bear almost any how."

In the spirit of Nietzsche's words, the following exercise, "Pebbles and Balls, Buttons and Beer," encapsulates the importance of having a why, and of letting your sense of why inspire your behavior. I have adapted this guided imagery exercise—different versions can readily be found on the Internet—to fit the world of education leaders, particularly school principals working with teachers. It can work equally well with all kinds of staff.

In real life, I invite you not only to use this exercise as described, but also to consider actually doing it in front of your staff and seeing if it works for them—and for you. As an alternative, you can do this exercise in the privacy of your office or home, using it as a reminder just for you.

PEBBLES AND BALLS, BUTTONS AND BEER
(10–15 minutes)

M

Try to imagine yourself in the situation described below, as if it were really happening to you. Be playful, and suspend disbelief for just a moment.

Imagine you are a principal in a school district near the North Carolina seashore and it's the first day back for teachers in late August. In keeping with the school's traditions, you're about to formally welcome the faculty back from vacation as well as try to set the tone for the school year ahead. Even though most of the teachers just finished busy summer jobs, they seem happy and eager to start, perhaps because they also squeezed in a little time at the ocean beaches and even played some golf.

Instead of starting the faculty meeting with your timeworn opening address, you've decided to try something completely new. After your greetings, you invite the faculty to engage in a thought experiment involving a large empty glass jar, which you have placed on a table at the front of the room. You also point to a big button pinned to your blazer with the inscription Viva VIA! You explain your hope for the time together—namely, to use the jar and the button to get them thinking about what matters the most to them and about their priorities for the school year ahead. You explain that VIA means values-inspired action, and you hope the practice will be long-lived.

A bit confused, but curious, the teachers agree, a little reluctantly, to go along. Relieved, you start by reaching under the table, pulling out a basket of golf balls, and carefully put them into the jar until it is filled. You ask the teachers, "Is the jar full?" They nod their heads. You then reach under the table and pull out a box of pebbles from a nearby beach parking lot. You pour the pebbles into the glass jar, shake the jar so they fill in the spaces between the golf balls, and then fill the jar to the brim with additional pebbles. You ask the teachers again, "Is the jar full?" They nod again, this time looking a bit baffled.

Again, you reach under the table, display a bag filled with beach sand, and pour it into the jar, filling the remaining spaces to the very top. "Is the jar finally full?" you ask the teachers, who agree unanimously, but appear still unsure about what's going on. Finally, you reach under the table, pull out two bottles of Budweiser, and slowly add the beer to the jar, soaking the sand and filling the empty spaces around it. The teachers laugh, beginning to go with the flow.

Now you say to the faculty, "I want you to imagine that the contents of the jar represent your priorities for the school year ahead. The golf balls represent your values, what really matters to you—things like pursuing excellence, caring for your students and colleagues, making room for family and friends—the big stuff that, if all else were lost, would still fill your life.

"The pebbles represent other things that matter, but not so much in the grander scheme of things—things like getting a bigger classroom, a fancier smartphone, a faster car to get to work. The sand is everything else, the small stuff, the often inconsequential activities that can fritter away much of your time without you even knowing it. Things like hanging out in the teachers' room, daydreaming, surfing the Internet.

"So, here's the big takeaway: you need to pursue balance in your life. If you put the sand into your jar first, there'll be no room for the pebbles, much less the golf balls. If you spend all your time and energy on the smaller stuff of life, you'll never get to the big stuff, doing the things that really matter to you. So, please remember this—take care of the golf balls first; the rest is mostly sand.

"And remember this, too—however full your life may seem, there's always room after school for a couple of Buds with family and friends."

At the end of the exercise, you thank your dear colleagues for their attention and then open up this first faculty meeting of the year for discussion. To get things rolling, you could hand out Viva VIA! buttons and distribute the leftover six packs . . . of golf balls. With a smile, you lead a spirited conversation about going for what matters.

M

Yield to Now

> Remember then: there is only one time
> that is important—Now! It is the most
> important time because it is the only
> time when we have any power.
>
> —*Leo Tolstoy*

In a Nutshell ...

What This Step Is

- The ability to *slow down and focus your attention* on the present moment, instead of racing through life driven by unhelpful thoughts about the past and the future

What This Step Helps You Do

- Become fully engaged in your experiences—and more aware of your strong and weak points, your unhelpful habits, and your blind spots
- Hone a calm, clear, stable, and flexible mind that can direct and sustain its attention and shift it away from resistance, rumination, and self-rebuke when necessary
- Live life intentionally, know experience directly, maintain an even keel, and appreciate the joys of life

THERE, BUT MOSTLY NOT THERE

Whenever I have the chance, I love to ride my bike along the Charles River, a beautiful ten-mile jaunt that begins about a mile from my home in Cambridge, Massachusetts, and takes me to Boston and back. If ever there was a place to be in the here and now, taking in the beauty moment by moment, this is the place for me: the sight of the Boston skyline, the sound of the rowers on the river, the smell of spring flowers, the touch of wind on my face, and, in the winter, the taste of salt on my lips from icy roads nearby.

Before I started to learn about mindfulness, when I went for a bike ride along the river, I was there, but mostly not there. I would take in the sights and sounds for a moment, but then my wandering mind took over. In fact, some days I could ride the entire trip on autopilot. I was vaguely aware of where I was, enough to avoid running over a baby carriage, but my mind was off somewhere else pondering this and that, often caught up in daydreaming and rumination.

When I first started to practice mindfulness, I aspired to someday do my bike ride totally in the moment, constantly smelling the roses. Within a minute or less, however, my mind was typically off and running—and often that's still true today, even after years of practicing mindfulness. Old habits are hard to break, and unrealistic aspirations are hard to meet.

But in important ways, things are different today from when I started. For one thing, I expect my mind to wander and don't beat myself up when it does; I watch its shenanigans with a sense of awe and I've given up trying to control what I cannot totally control. For another thing, I catch myself sooner, when I'm there in body but not in mind, and bring my attention back to the sights and sounds of the ride. Moreover, because it's easy to forget to be mindful, I've learned to use physical waypoints—bridges, intersections, crosswalks, stairs—as reminders to turn toward my current experiences. In my mind's eye, I visualize these way-points as yield signs that tell me to slow down and give way to opposing traffic, so to speak—in this case, give way to being present in the moment.

I've also developed a more nuanced view of mind wandering: woolgathering is not all bad. I keep a lookout for unhelpful wan-derings, particularly those that magnify my stress and under-mine my focus on what matters most to me. For example, if I notice I'm worrying about something for the umpteenth time, I'll bring my attention back to the sights and sounds of my ride. Or if I notice that I'm beating myself up, I'll bring my attention back to the here and now. On the other hand, if I notice that my mind is off somewhere joyfully brainstorming a current work problem, or perhaps happily rehearsing a class I'm about to teach, or even doing some pleasurable—and harmless—daydreaming, I may not yield to the present moment and instead fully engage in this mind wandering.

Y

As you see, I'm neither dogmatic about the application of this step of MY DANCE in every situation nor averse to all forms of mind wandering. Moreover, this step of being in the here and now is not easy to learn. But being present is really important. Even though we can't totally control our attention, we can guide it in ways that can be quite helpful, as this chapter will show.

As I write this chapter, it is a bright, sunny morning, and I'm hoping to go for a bike ride soon. I plan to attend to the sights and sounds, monitor my attention, and bring my atten-tion back over and over again when my mind wanders off, as it will. For sure, I intend to detect and disrupt those wanderings that are unhelpful, but I just might stay with any stimulating mental forays that give me wholesome pleasure. I plan to attend to my current experiences and simultaneously be open to go with the flow.

WHAT LIES AHEAD

In chapter 5, we focused on how to define your values and put them into action so that you can lead a richer and more meaningful life as an education leader. We now turn to mindfulness, which MY DANCE presents mainly as a means to an end—a set of practices that can help you handle your stress wisely and thereby avoid losing sight of what matters most to you. Indeed, mindfulness can be an antidote to the common human affliction of unintentionally getting in our own way. And, of course, mindfulness has numerous other benefits as well.

So what exactly is mindfulness, this ancient practice with contemplative roots that has recently gone viral in the modern world? There have been dozens of published definitions of mindfulness over the years, including Jon Kabat-Zinn's definition, cited earlier in the book.[1] Scientists and scholars well versed in mindfulness research tend to agree that there is no consensus definition.[2] My take on mindfulness has been shaped by fairly well known meditation teachers and clinicians who are credited with integrating mindfulness-based approaches into their practices and programs. (See "The Origins of MY DANCE" in chapter 3.)

I most often think of mindfulness as a special way of paying attention to enhance awareness. The first goal of mindfulness is to recognize *what* we pay attention to. We pay attention to the here and now, and this lies at the heart of mindfulness. Mindfulness encourages our minds to be focused on the present moment, instead of having our bodies in one place and our minds somewhere else, speeding along as they chew over the past and the future. You'd be amazed at what scientists have discovered about our mind-wandering habits: According to a 2010 Harvard study, people spend about 47 percent of their waking hours thinking about something other than what they're doing in the moment—and a wandering mind typically leads to unhappiness.[3] Mindfulness counters the mind's natural tendency to wander.

In the here and now, you pay attention to what you are *directly experiencing*. The object of your attention may be a body sensation, a thought, a feeling, or anything else you can hear, see, taste, touch, or smell. In my way of parsing mindfulness, this focus on the now is one of the three core elements of mindfulness and is the focus of this chapter.

This special way of paying attention entails intentionality, calmness, patience, and curiosity, instead of doing what our minds normally do, which is to judge, compare, rehash, worry, ignore whatever we are experiencing, or just wander off hither and yon. We also pay attention in two other important ways—from a distance, and with an openness to our experiences—two other core elements of mindfulness, which are examined in depth in later chapters.

Mindfulness can also be defined by what it is not. Paying attention speaks to *observing* our internal and external experiences as opposed to ruminating or excessively overthinking them. Instead of racing through life knowing the world through our hyperactive thinking minds, like speeding limousines on an expressway, we are being mindful when we put on the brakes and yield, turning our attention to what we experience directly through our five senses and through the observation of our thinking. Being mindful is different from being mind full.

Mindfulness is also the opposite of familiar everyday habits such as multitasking, getting lost in thought, daydreaming, operating on autopilot, or ruminating over what's bugging you. All of these behavior patterns are marked by the absence of careful observation of our direct experiences and thereby preclude mindful awareness.

And strange as it might sound, mindfulness is not a method directly aimed at making you feel better, but rather is aimed at making you better at watching—and learning from—your moment-to-moment feelings, thoughts, and body sensations. To be sure, practicing mindfulness often results in relaxation, which can be thought of as a beneficial by-product of this practice aimed at enhancing your awareness.

A mindfulness-based approach can help you master your attention—a central, yet often overlooked skill of effective leadership. No doubt, external constraints—for example, the expectation that you'll always be connected—affect where leaders place their attention. But the good news is that you can learn how to better guide your attention with significant payoffs, especially when it comes to your mind's response to difficult situations. Indeed, if you pay attention to attention and learn how to flexibly direct, sustain, shift, expand, and narrow your attention consciously, you will open your mind to new choices that can dramatically enhance your ability to flourish as a leader. "The faculty of voluntarily bringing back a wandering attention, over and over again, is the very root of judgment, character, and will," says William James, the father of modern psychology.[4]

LEARNING TO BE HERE AND NOW

It's one thing to read about mindfulness; it's quite another to learn how to make the practice part of your life. This requires actually experiencing mindfulness for yourself, so you can strengthen what can be thought of as a mental muscle—that is, your capacity to pay attention to the here and now and redirect your attention when it wanders unhelpfully—which is central to your conscious awareness and to your leadership. "Mindfulness is neither difficult nor complex," Christina Feldman reminds us, "remembering to be mindful is the great challenge."[5] Practice helps you remember.

In teaching this step during workshops, I often begin by using a flashlight in a darkened room to try to create a visceral sense of what directing and redirecting attention feels like, in an effort to address unhelpful—and helpful—mind wandering. In advance, I place half a dozen posters around the room with various labels: Task at Hand; Productive Thinking; Resisting; Ruminating; Rebuking; and Breathing. Here's a synopsis of what I do and say.

I start by asking participants to imagine that their attention is like the beam of a flashlight, which I hold in my hand. I aim the flashlight at the Task at Hand poster, saying that this might be, for example, a board of education meeting where they will be called on to make a presentation, with the beam of light illuminating the focus of their attention. I then demonstrate—by moving the beam in a zigzag fashion around the room—what often happens: their attention wanders from what they're doing.

Next, I suggest that mind wandering is not always a problem. For example, while you are waiting to present at the board meeting, suppose your mind wanders off to do some productive thinking. I demonstrate this situation by moving the beam of light to the Productive Thinking poster. Such mind wandering could be a good thing because it might include helpful activities such as planning for an upcoming project, thinking ahead to the rest of your day, or analyzing a problem you are wrestling with. In fact, in the face of a meandering board of education discussion, you might intentionally redirect your attention to productive thinking.

I then suggest that mind wandering, however, is often a significant problem, which I demonstrate by shining the light onto the Resisting, Ruminating, and Rebuking posters, one by one, adding a bit of commentary. For example, I use the flashlight to show how the focus may be on the board meeting, but your attention wanders off because your mind *resists* your frustrated feelings of being unprepared, it *ruminates* on the fear that you may be called out for being unprepared, and it *rebukes* you harshly for being unprepared. All of this mind wandering could undermine your upcoming presentation.

If you pay attention to where your beam of light is aimed, I suggest, you are then able to do three things: (1) detect when your attention has wandered unhelpfully; (2) make a mental note of this wandering (indeed, you might even say to yourself, for the fun of it, "There you go again," to borrow a famous line from President Ronald Reagan); and then (3) bring your attention back to the task at hand. What's more, if your mind is particularly unstable and unfocused, you might focus on breathing, taking a few breaths to anchor yourself in the present moment. This process of beaming in on an object of attention and repeatedly bringing the light back when it wanders is exactly what happens in much of mindfulness training.

FORMAL PRACTICES TO DEVELOP MINDFULNESS

At its base, mindfulness can be cultivated through formal contemplative practices such as meditation (as well as yoga, tai chi, and the martial arts) and through a multitude of informal practices and experiential activities, which I'll turn to in a moment. Formal meditations entail the conscious focusing of attention in one of three ways:

- single-pointed concentration on a particular object you choose, such as the breath, body sensations, movements like walking, sounds, and sights (often called *focused awareness* in the research literature)
- an open and receptive focus on your immediate experiences— what's happening right now in your mind, your body, or your environment (often called *open monitoring*)
- a focus on wholesome thoughts and feelings that cultivate positive attitudes toward yourself and others—for example, altruism, compassion, and gratitude (often known as *mettā*, a Pali word for kindness, benevolence, and compassion-based meditations)

On the following pages, I spell out three formal practices that focus on the breath, sounds, and, of all things, the soles of your feet. If you're interested in getting more deeply into formal meditation, there are countless meditation recordings easily accessible on the Internet and elsewhere. I have listened for years to guided meditations by Jon Kabat-Zinn. If you're new to meditation, I recommend his book, *Mindfulness for Beginners*, which includes a CD of taped meditations.[6] Also, see "Further Readings and Resources" at the end of the book.

A good place to start formal practice is with mindful breathing, which can enhance your ability to stay present by stilling your mind, calming your body, and opening your heart. I start with the breath because it's the most popular object of attention in formal meditation—in fact, people have been meditating by paying attention to their breathing for more than twenty-five hundred years. In this type of concentration meditation, the basic instructions are threefold: (1) chose a neutral object of attention (in this case, the breath), (2) direct your attention and sustain your focus on this object, and (3) when your mind wanders, as it will, gently bring your attention back to the chosen object, over and over and over again. It's safe to say that at this very moment, thousands upon thousands of people around the globe are engaged in mindful breathing.

The exercise "Mindful Breathing" is a bare-bones version of this breathing practice, which can be done for just a few minutes, or for much longer if you have the time and inclination. Remember that the more you practice, the more you are strengthening your attention muscle.

MINDFUL BREATHING   *(10–15 minutes)*

Take a moment to slow down and get ready in a way that works for you.

When you are ready, direct your attention to your breathing. Start by slowing your breathing down, and simply notice it as you breathe in . . . and breathe out. Notice your breath as if you are noticing it for the very first time. Notice its natural rhythm as you breathe in . . . and breathe out. There's nothing to do except notice your breath.

When your mind wanders, as it will, no problem. Just notice its wanderings and gently return your attention to your breathing. Simply fall into this pattern, pay attention to your breath, and when you detect that your attention has been diverted, gently bring it back to the breath, over and over again . . .

Finally, when you are ready, gradually widen your attention to the room around you, and gently open your eyes with the intention of bringing this focus on the here and now to your experiences throughout the day.

There are several things you can do to enhance your concentration and the experience of this basic breathing exercise. Here are four you might try as you develop your practice:

- You can more narrowly concentrate your attention on a specific part of the breathing process, for example, the rise and fall of your belly as you breathe in and out, or the cool air as it enters your nostrils and the warm air as you exhale.
- You can add words silently spoken to yourself. For example, on the in-breath, you might say, "Now, I'm breathing in"; on the out-breath, "Now, I'm breathing out." Or, you might say on the in-breath words like "Calm"; on the out-breath, "Peace."
- You might count your breaths by silently saying "One" as you exhale your first out-breath, "two" on the second out-breath, and so on, up to "ten"; when your mind wanders, begin again at "One."
- When your mind wanders, you might notice and name where it wanders—"Ah, there's a thought"; or "There's a memory"; or "There's frustration."

The idea is to experiment with these enhancements and see what works for you.

For some people, a focus on the breath can be difficult, particularly for those new to meditation. Also, a focus on breathing can be difficult for those with respiratory problems. So, here are two alternatives you might explore—first a focus on sounds followed by a focus on the soles of your feet—which are adapted from the work of psychologist Susan Pollak and her collaborators.[7] You can get ready for the meditation as you did with the breathing exercise, or you can adopt any variation that helps you become comfortable, relaxed, alert, and aware. This exercise is an easy and direct way to yield to now.

Y

SOUNDS GALORE *(5–10 minutes)*

When you're ready, begin to listen to the sounds that surround you. Just listen. See if you can listen with your entire being. Just notice the sounds.

You might notice the sound of a fan, a passing car, a shuffle in the back of the room, a ticking watch.

You don't need to do anything special or force anything. Just let yourself settle in and listen. Listen to the sounds. Listen to the silence. Let what you hear be the focus of your attention.

If your mind wanders, welcome to the club. That's what minds do. They fret about the past, worry about the future. They daydream. Fantasize. Compare. Obsess. Criticize. Judge. When your hyperactive mind wanders, just bring your attention back to the sounds surrounding you. Over and over again.

If you get distracted, no problem. No reason for self-criticism. Just start over again—and notice the sounds around you. Just listening.

When you are ready to stop, wiggle your fingers and toes, stretch, and open your eyes (if they've been closed) with the intention of bringing this awareness to the rest of your day.

Since newcomers to mindfulness often assume that meditation requires being seated—ideally, on a cushion on the floor—it helps to dispel this notion early on and demystify the practice. What's essential is not your exact body position, but just noticing what you intend to notice, with your body and mind in the same room. In the next exercise, "'Soleful' Standing," the invitation is to stand and to focus your attention mainly on the soles of your feet. Ideally, you might practice in a quiet place where you won't be disturbed for, say, five minutes or so. It's also a good practice in informal settings, for instance, while standing in a line or while waiting at a train station. Again, fit the length to the time you have.

"SOLEFUL" STANDING   (5–10 minutes)

Stand up, and take a moment to get comfortable. Stand in an erect position that's both relaxed and alert. Close your eyes, if you like. Have your feet flat on the floor, your hands by your side. Let yourself become fully grounded in the earth. Aware of your insides—and your outside environment. Be present in this moment. Right here. Right now.

When you are ready, raise a hand and wiggle your fingers. Notice the sensations in your hand. This is what mindfulness is all about. Knowing what you are experiencing when you are experiencing it.

Now, if you are willing, stretch your arms above your head, stretching them as far as you can without hurting yourself, as if you were reaching for the stars. As you stretch, notice any body sensations. Notice any accompanying thoughts and feelings. Just notice your experiences. Mindfulness is just knowing what you are doing while you are doing it.

When you are ready, lower your arms, and switch your attention to the soles of your feet, as if your mind were a powerful flashlight that you could control. Just notice the sensations of your feet on the ground.

If you like, you can stomp your feet and make some noise. As you do so, notice your body sensations and what you hear. Also, notice your self-talk. Your mind might be saying something like this: "This is not what I expected. Where are the robes and incense?"

Now, you can shift your body forward and back, then side to side. Let yourself feel rooted, solid, connected to the earth. See if you can find your balance and come into your center. Try to stay over your feet.

Now take a few breaths, and know that you are standing. Feel the soles of your feet. You don't need to do anything special, just keep bringing your attention back to the sensations of your feet on the ground. Let yourself feel grounded. Anchored to the earth.

When your mind wanders, smile at this wondrous thought machine, and just bring your attention back to the soles of your feet.

Finally, if it feels comfortable, broaden and shift your attention from your feet to your whole body, as if you were widening the beam of a flashlight. Notice any places that feel tight or tense, and invite those places to soften. Notice where you are relaxed. No need to fix anything, just acknowledge it, without judgment, with kind attention. Let yourself be in your body for a moment or so.

When you are ready to stop, wiggle your fingers and toes, stretch, and return to what you were doing with the intention of bringing this awareness to the rest of your day.

Y

INFORMAL PRACTICES TO DEVELOP MINDFULNESS

A concern many education leaders express is the lack of time for formal meditation, not to mention the absence of a special place to meditate at a special time. As the above exercises suggest, practice need not take a long time. Moreover, one way to practice daily that takes no extra time at all is to do your daily routines in a mindful way. So, for example, instead of taking a shower with your mind on your to-do list, for the first minute bring your full attention to your five senses—the touch of hot water on your body, the sound of rushing water, the smell of the shampoo, and so on. You can be similarly mindful in other everyday activities, like eating, driving, brushing your teeth, walking your dog.

There's growing evidence that these informal practices can make a difference. For example, one recent study found that people who washed dishes mindfully (by focusing on smelling the soap, feeling the water heat, and touching the dishes) lowered their nervousness levels by 27 percent, whereas the control group showed no benefits at all.[8] The idea is to do one thing at a time and to try to avoid getting hijacked by your mind, which is ever eager to yank you away from direct experiences.

Another alternative to formal practice is to build short pauses into your schedule (e.g., see the "Morning ABCs" exercise in chapter 11). I also try to pause several times a day to take as little as three deep breaths. To help me remember to pause, I rely on the ring of a mindfulness bell when working at my computer.[9]

DETECTING AND DISRUPTING RUMINATION

It turns out that paying attention to the here and now is an especially effective response to the unhelpful habit of ruminating, that is, the obsessive, negative, and self-absorbed thinking about the past and the future. Undue rumination, which is different from productive thinking, can appear like a bolt out of the blue or be triggered by what's upsetting you and by your attempts to fix the problem. "Since neurons that fire together wire together," neuropsychologist Rick Hanson says, "staying with a negative experience past the point that's useful is like running laps in Hell: You dig the track a little deeper in your brain each time you go around it."[10] Being right here, right now, is helpful because you cannot simultaneously ruminate over past misdeeds and future mishaps—a major preoccupation when ruminating—and mindfully focus on what your senses are telling you about the present.

With practice, you can learn to interrupt downward spirals of negative thoughts.[11] Indeed, you can train your mind to notice when you are obsessed with the past and the future—or when you are triggered by upsetting experiences and on the verge of automatically starting to ruminate. We can develop what Buddhist teacher Joseph Goldstein calls an "inner remote control" that can change channels.[12] In other words, when you become aware of ruminating, you can disrupt the process by redirecting your attention to the present moment, thereby precluding time travel to the past and future—the mind can only be in one time zone at a time. When your mind wanders back to rumination, gently bring it back to the here and now, over and over again.[13]

In the next exercise, "Five-Sense Pause," for example, you imagine yourself sitting in your office between meetings rehashing a bad morning (during which you discussed the declining college budget with the senior faculty at your college) and worrying about the upheavals to come that afternoon (when you will meet with two faculty members who have not been granted tenure). Of course, this exercise can be adapted to a wide variety of circumstances. The aim of the exercise is to help you reduce your rumination by getting in contact with the present moment by paying attention to your five senses.

FIVE-SENSE PAUSE (3–5 minutes)

When you are ready, turn your attention to your five senses, cataloging what they are taking in right now, one by one, for about thirty seconds each. Follow this general protocol: Say to yourself, "Right now I am seeing —— [fill in the blank]," "Right now I am hearing ——," and so on, for smell, taste, and tactile sensations you are experiencing both inside and outside your body. And when your mind wanders, bring your attention back to whatever sense you are attending to.

Specifically, you might say something like this to yourself: "Right now, I'm seeing the new couch in my office, the full wastepaper basket under my desk, the picture of my parrot on the table. Right now, I'm hearing the buzz of the air conditioner, the chatter outside my door, my stomach gurgling. Right now, I smell the remains of my morning coffee, the lemon floor polish, the aroma of leather. Right now, I taste toothpaste, the lingering flavor of a spicy lunch.

"Now, I notice that my mind has wandered back to this morning's troubling meeting, so I'm gently bringing my mind back to what I taste. Right now, I sense the dryness in my mouth. Finally, right now, I notice the touch of my socks against my skin, the chair under my thighs, the heaviness in my stomach."

When you've finished going through each of your five senses, gradually widen your attention to the room around you with the intention of bringing this focus on the here and now to your meetings this afternoon.

The foregoing meditation can be a helpful time-out from rumination. What's more, once you go through this exercise, sense by sense, you are less likely to return to your rehashing and fretting.

Bringing nonjudgmental awareness to your physical reality in the moment not only can help you with rumination but can also be quite nourishing by providing pleasure (see chapter 9, "Nourish Yourself"). As a prelude to that discussion, consider taking a moment now to concentrate on each of your senses and how they nourish you. Contemplate three things for each of your senses, for fifteen observations in all.

Here's my list. *Sight:* family photos, a splash of sunflowers, my dog's wagging tail. *Smell:* Camembert cheese, the fragrance of lilacs, a French boulangerie. *Sound:* birds chirping at dawn, a Puccini opera, my pet geese honking. *Taste:* recently picked corn, a homemade strawberry-rhubarb cobbler, a ripe peach. *Touch:* a massage, a bubble bath, a warm sweater. I invite you to savor what the senses have to offer.

A more playful and unorthodox approach to dealing with rumination, inspired by a talk by Joseph Goldstein at the Cambridge Insight Meditation Center, is the "Six-Shooter Retort," an experiential exercise that can be quickly done.[14] It is designed to help you use your imagination and sense of humor to stop an oncoming bout of rumination in its tracks. (If you find any mention of guns offensive, you might want to skip this exercise.)

SIX-SHOOTER RETORT *(1–2 minutes)*

Take a moment to check in and notice whether your mind is engaged in unhelpful rumination. If so, take another moment to pause and get ready to make use of your imagination.

Now, imagine you are the marshal, Riot Burp, in a Wild West frontier town, on the lookout for the notorious Ruminator Gang. Patrolling Main Street, you witness the boss of the gang, Arnold Sportshager, galloping toward you with a pistol in his hand. Imagine drawing your trusty Colt .45 six-shooter from your holster. You give it a twirl and stop the gunslinger cold with a single warning shot above his head. For dramatic effect, imagine whiffing away the smoke at the tip of your gun barrel as you turn toward the bystanders. Now, open your eyes and imagine smugly smiling at the starstruck crowd as you swagger off.

Might you try this lighthearted approach to being present and dealing with a bout of rumination? Does it work for you? Might you invent your very own approach?

BENEFITS OF BEING MINDFUL

The practice of mindfulness not only can strengthen your bedrock awareness and counteract rumination, but can also enhance your leadership in many important ways. "A leader tuned out of his internal world will be rudderless," says psychologist and author Daniel Goleman. "One blind to the world of others will be clueless; those indifferent to the larger systems within which they operate will be blindsided."[15]

Mindfulness has many benefits for leaders.[16] First of all, being present is at the heart of self-awareness because it anchors you in the reality of the moment. This state of mind is crucial for leaders, who can easily get lost in their ambitious plans and thereby lose sight of reality, delude themselves about their accomplishments, and otherwise fall victim to hubris in solving problems. While not diminishing big dreams, self-awareness promotes oft-needed humility—and a willingness to face reality.

Being present also stabilizes and calms the mind and, in doing so, fosters *situational awareness*, which is essential to being an effective leader. As you become better at mastering your attention, instead of being preoccupied or easily distracted, you can perceive—with greater clarity, objectivity, and an open mind—your outer and inner experiences as each moment occurs. You are thereby able to size up the situation and make wiser real-time decisions.

Paying attention to the present moment is also the key ingredient in *task engagement*, that is, the ability to focus your mind's eye like a laser on the leadership work at hand and quickly regain your concentration when you are unhelpfully distracted. Task engagement is no easy task, of course, in a society that values and even requires multitasking.[17] Paul E. Flaxman and his colleagues explain why such engagement is important: "A focus on the present is particularly important because that is where new learning occurs and where the value-oriented opportunities afforded by the environment are discovered."[18]

Additionally, being present and fully engaged in the work of your colleagues is essential to developing good working relationships. Coworkers will be put off if they sense you are present physically but not mentally or if your mind tends to wander off in the middle of a discussion. Indeed, it's hard to exaggerate the importance of being fully there when you meet with others and of listening with empathy as if nothing else in the world is more important to you in that moment. Sometimes, just showing up as a caring human being is all you can do as an education leader.

Another benefit of paying attention to the present moment is that it opens your eyes to the magnificent richness of life as we live it, with all its joys and sorrows, pleasures and pain. You live life in the present, in your moment-to-moment experiences. Not in the past. Not in the future. You miss out on much of what life has to offer if you constantly sleepwalk through your limited days on earth with your body in one place and your mind surfing the past and the future. As you become better at mastering your attention, you develop the capacity to choose wholesome experiences as the objects of your attention, which can provide a source of daily nourishment.

Finally, the ability to be fully present is essential in developing a broad perspective on who you are, on your relationship with your thoughts and feelings as they come and go, and on how to manage the emotional roller coaster of leadership life. These are the subjects I now turn to in chapter 7.

CHAPTER SEVEN

D isentangle from Upsets

The greatest griefs are those we cause ourselves.

—Sophocles

In a Nutshell ...

What This Step Is

- The ability to *step back*, *observe*, and *make room* for upsets, as well as the ability to *be with* upsets, instead of *being* them

What This Step Helps You Do

- Counter the normal human tendency to fully identify with upsetting thoughts and feelings—a tendency that is a root cause of emotional difficulties

- Access a part of your mind with the capacity to shine the light of awareness on upsetting thoughts and feelings, thereby providing a broader perspective on what's troubling you

- Hold upsets more lightly, take them less personally, and just watch them come and go

IN HIS HAT!

Rain or shine, some thirty-two thousand graduates, alumni, family, and guests gather each spring on the central green of Harvard Yard for the university-wide commencement exercises. Facing the audience and sitting under a big tent, university officials, civic dignitaries, faculty, and honorees assemble on a stone platform at the steps of Memorial Church, most wearing formal morning dress or academic robes topped with a hat called a tam. The gathering is called to order by the sheriff of Middlesex County, who arrives on horseback. Shortly thereafter, the chaplain of the day offers a prayer.

While I was dean, the chaplain was Peter Gomes, a revered member of the Harvard community greatly admired for his oratorical skills. Upon the call of the university marshal, Reverend Gomes, clad in a flowing gown, would rise and unhurriedly approach the podium, which was positioned directly in front of the row of deans. He would carefully remove his tam, solemnly bow his head, and deliver a beautifully worded prayer. Little did I know until I sat right behind him that he was reading from notes hidden in his hat!

At first sight, I was stunned, but also relieved and inspired. It had never occurred to me that a speaker of his distinction and eloquence would rely on notes, much less cleverly carry them in his hat. I was relieved because obviously he, like me, devoted enormous time and energy to being well prepared. And I was inspired to use my hat in a similar way on Commencement Day in the years to come.

If truth be told, commencement was always a nerve-wracking experience for me as I awaited my turn to speak. I'd sit there smiling, looking out over the huge crowd as if I had not a worry in the world. On the inside, however, I was fretting about going blank—or doing a belly flop as I walked across the platform to present the graduates of the School of Education to the president of the university. Thanks to Reverend Gomes, I was prepared. If I forgot my words, I could lower my gaze and read them, written out in big letters and taped to the inside of my tam. I then returned to my seat, took a deep sigh of relief, and began to experience the pure pleasure of graduation time.

LOOKING BACK—AND FORWARD

So far, we have focused on paying attention to our attention, so to speak, so we can purposely observe our experiences open-mindedly, detect when our minds are wandering unhelpfully, and redirect our attention back to here-and-now experiences. Remember my flashlight activity? In that exercise, the mind's awareness was represented by a flashlight's beam of light, which can focus on a variety of mental contents, including the three Rs: resisting, ruminating, and rebuking.

In this chapter, the focus shifts from the what and how of observing your experiences to exploring the very part of your mind that's aware and observing. In other words, we'll start contemplating the flashlight itself. It's the part of the human mind that's one step removed from your experiences, the part that's conscious of your consciousness.

This aspect of us, which I call our Light, can be accessed by learning to disentangle from the contents of your mind—that is, by mentally separating from the thoughts and feelings that are there.[1] What I call disentangling and my Light are implicit in mindfulness practices, but I make them explicit here because I believe that this elaboration will enhance your capacity to constructively handle upsets.

As we will see, showing up in life as your Light is quite helpful because the part of you that's aware of your experiences can be neither hurt nor harmed by the upsetting contents of your mind. You may be experiencing upsetting thoughts, for example, but the part of your mind that's aware of your upsets—your

D

Light—is not upset; it is just aware. Or you may be experiencing punishing stress, but your Light is not stressed; it is just aware. Your Light has the capacity to illuminate your experiences so that you can *be* with them instead of *being* them; the difference can have a profoundly positive effect on how you handle upsets.

Because it's easier to experience these unfamiliar ideas than to explain them in everyday language, let me elaborate— and emphasize several experiential exercises. In a moment, I'll explore the upsetting thoughts that regularly tumble out of our minds and how we often mishandle them by overidentifying with them. I then examine disentangling—what it means, how to do it, and what its benefits are—and along the way explore the qualities of your Light.

But first, the inspiration for the term my Light: It's adapted from a beautiful song in the album *Songversation*, by an American singer-songwriter and musician named India.Arie, who captures in her lyrics the essence of this chapter—namely, that we are a lot more than all the troubling thoughts and feelings in our life; at our core, we are that aspect of our mind that can step back and cast the light of awareness on our experiences. Here's an excerpt:

> *I am light, I am light*
> *I am light, I am light*
> *I am light, I am light*
> *I am light, I am light*
> *I am not the things my family did*
> *I am not the voices in my head*
> *I am not the pieces of the brokenness inside*
>
> *I am light, I am light*
> *I am light, I am light*
> *I am light, I am light*
> *I am light, I am light*

I'm not the mistakes that I have made or any of the
*   things that caused me pain*
I am not the pieces of the dream I left behind

I am light, I am light
I am light, I am light
I am light, I am light
I am light, I am light
I am not the color of my eyes
I am not the skin on the outside
I am not my age, I am not my race, my soul inside
*   is all light*

All light, all light
All light, all light
I am light, I am light[2]

CHATTERING MIND

As elaborated upon earlier, we humans constantly think; we're thinking more than we could ever imagine. In the privacy of our hyperactive minds, we evaluate, compare, scold ourselves, plan, worry, and so on. Even though we chatter away to ourselves during much of our waking hours, we don't often think about our thinking or watch ourselves do it. To be sure, this ability to use language and thereby think is one of our greatest strengths, distinguishing humans from other sentient beings. But constant self-talk can also be a source of difficulties, especially when we identify too closely with our troubling thoughts and become one with them.

To experience viscerally just how busy, scattered, and even zany our minds can be, I invite you to experience the following exercise, adapted from acceptance and commitment therapy.[3] It requires you to work with someone else, perhaps your partner, a friend, or just someone you get to volunteer; I promise they will enjoy it. Indeed, the exercise works really well in group settings and allows for a lively after-exercise discussion.

Besides being fun, the experience illuminates how our chattering minds undermine our ability both to deal with troubling situations and to live life fully. The following exercise, "Walking with Your Mind," includes time for reflection. If you turn it into a group exercise, it calls for a facilitator to monitor the time. The instructions are written to accommodate a group, but can easily be modified to accommodate a single pair.

WALKING WITH YOUR MIND   *(20–30 minutes)*

To start, identify a partner for the duration of this exercise. One member of each pair will assume the role of the "person"; the other will be the person's "mind." After about three minutes, you will switch roles with your partner.

As the "person," your job is threefold: (1) take a walk in any direction you choose; (2) notice what's happening in you and around you, focusing on your physical experiences—what you see, hear, smell, feel; and (3) listen to your "mind" (your partner), but don't communicate with "it."

If you are the "mind," your job is to follow your person (your partner) around as if you were a chirpy bird on his or her shoulder—close up and personal. As you walk about, *talk constantly and loudly*—compare, plan, warn, evaluate, encourage, worry, scold, cajole—do the things our chattering minds do.

For example, if you were a university president, your hyperactive mind might babble along like this: "I can't believe I'm doing this exercise when I could be home working on my vision; you're the worst president in the state; I'm really pissed off at the reaction to my opening address; where are you walking—don't you have any sense of direction?—you are such a dunce when it comes to fundraising; the junior faculty is driving me crazy with their demands for more tenure slots; I'm worried about the enrollment shortfall; it's time you shape up and stop acting like a wonky professor; now just relax, everything is going to be hunky-dory."

So, that's the exercise. Now, find a partner, choose your starting roles, and take your mind for a walk for about three minutes. Then switch roles for about three minutes. After that, there will be time for individual and, if appropriate, group reflection and discussion.

When you complete the role-playing, take a few minutes to reflect on the overall experience. What was it like? What did you notice? How did it feel? What effect did your chattering mind have on your ability to physically experience your world? To concentrate? To do what you wanted to do? What did you learn?

D

In my experience, this exercise really hits home with education leaders. Besides being amused, you may well see, perhaps for the first time, just how busy your mind can be and how your thoughts can interfere with—even undermine—what you want to do. You may begin to understand what psychologist Steven Hayes means when he says we need to "put the mind on a leash."

HANDLING UPSETTING THOUGHTS

When we are facing difficult and unsettling situations, it's not unusual for us to become entangled with a cascade of emotionally charged, negative thoughts and feelings—about ourselves and about others. Here's an example of how negative thoughts can spiral downward: Thoughts such as "I'm angry" can devolve to "I'm an angry person," to "I'm an unfit leader," and, ultimately, to "I'm such a loser." One can also imagine a similar pattern of self-deprecating thoughts about being frightened, ashamed, sad, misunderstood—and so on.

So, here's the problem. If our minds regularly spew out a flood of negative self-evaluations, it's easy to identify with them as the whole of who we are. It's easy to fall into the trap of thinking, "I *am* my negative thoughts"; "I *am* my disabling emotions"; "I *am* the aches in my body"; "I *am* just a bundle of upsetting reactions." This aspect of us might be labeled the Entangled Mind, because it feels as if we are totally tied up by our problems. In our mind's eye, we end up *being* our upsets, which sets us up for being totally self-absorbed and taking all our stuff personally. In this state, we tend to react rashly and automatically—like a reflex—with little conscious control.

To oversimplify, consider two parts of our minds. One part, familiar to us, experiences upsets and is inclined to get entangled with them. The less familiar part of our minds is aware that we are experiencing upsets, but is not upset by the upsets it is observing. "The mind is, in fact, capable of examining what is happening within it," Matthieu Ricard reminds us. "All we need to do is observe our emotions in the same way we would observe an external event taking place in front of us . . . [A]wareness is not affected by the emotion it is observing. When we understand that, we can step back, realize that the emotion has no solidity and allow enough space for it to dissolve by itself."[4]

In "Blinded by Hands," a short exercise adapted from the work of Russ Harris, the hands are used as a metaphor for the problem of overidentification with upsetting thoughts and feelings, which in turn can undermine leadership.[5]

BLINDED BY HANDS *(3–5 minutes)*

Start by doing two things: First, imagine you are at a meeting of your top staff—for example, a school district's academic cabinet, which consists of the chairs of various academic departments and the district's chief administrative officers. Second, imagine that your hands contain all your difficult thoughts, emotions, and memories—all the heavy stuff that you keep stewing over and that keeps you awake at night.

Now, slowly bring your hands up toward your face, with the palms together and facing you, until your hands cover your eyes. Now that you are blinded by your hands, blinded by all your heavy stuff, ponder these questions: Am I aware of what's happening in the academic cabinet meeting? Do I feel connected to my colleagues around me? Can I do those things I value—for example, interact with my colleagues, concentrate on the district's budget, exercise leadership? Notice that when you are totally entangled in your heavy stuff, you miss out on a lot. Your attention is not on the meeting. You are disconnected from the world around you. You cannot do those things that maximize your performance. You forget about the things that matter most to you.

When you are ready, slowly bring your attention back to the room and return to the day ahead.

D

Many leaders who identify with upsets resort to some combination of the three Rs to free themselves from discomfort: They resist reality and take impulsive or self-destructive steps to fix the problem. They ruminate unduly over upsets and rebuke themselves for falling short. Wholly entangled with their thoughts and emotions, they show up in an agitated state, often responding reflexively with unhelpful actions. They yell, hide, lash out, and make ill-informed snap decisions. To themselves and others, these leaders appear to be nothing more than a bundle of inappropriate overreactions.

So, you may ask, what's the alternative to overidentifying with my upsets? Well, you can learn to be with them by taking a mental step away from them, thereby providing some space to relate to them in a different way. Instead of being entangled with upsets, you can develop a new perspective by making room for them and observing them from a distance.

In much more vibrant language, a friend of mine, Heidi Fischbach, a masseuse and a writer, captures the essence of what I'm talking about in a recent essay, "Alone in the Cafeteria," which is aimed at all of us who at times feel lonely:

> Everyone knows the alone in the cafeteria feeling. Even people who never sat alone in the cafeteria know the alone in the cafeteria feeling.
>
> You wake up early and find alone in the cafeteria camped out on your chest. You would kick it out but you know it would only come back tomorrow having changed its clothes. And since even in a new purple ruffle hopscotch bikini everyone knows alone in the cafeteria, today you say hello.
>
> Anyone sitting here? it asks.
>
> You are, you say, scooching over to make room.[6]

Disentangling from upsets is really about scooching over to make room.

In more formal terms, this process of scooching over, says David Rome, founder of Mindful Focusing, can be described in multiple ways: "stepping back from the emotion, placing the emotion somewhere outside of you, rising above the emotion, making yourself larger than the emotion, or putting a box around the emotion."[7] As Rome says, knowing how to create this room between us and our upsets "is a skill vital to our long-term welfare."

This process allows us not only to separate from the contents of our minds, but also to show up as that part of our minds that can act like a calm, curious, and objective scientist watching our inside dramas from the outside. From this vantage point, which can be cultivated through the practice of mindfulness, we can be with our upsets in a particular way—noticing them, acknowledging them, and making space for them—instead of being our upsets, totally entangled, defined, and consumed by them. I call this process *disentangling* to capture a visceral sense of the struggle to pull apart from a messy tangle.

There's no good label in everyday language for the part of your mind that's a step removed from your upsetting thoughts and feelings. I call it my Light, as I mentioned earlier, but you can call it whatever you like—or not give it a name at all. Indeed, a number of ancient wisdom traditions, as well as modern psychotherapies, have given different names—for example, Pure Awareness, the Self, Observing Self, Self-in-Presence—to this special, hard-to-describe capacity for awareness within us.

D

The label is less important than the basic insight: we humans all have a part of our minds that can shine a bright light on our experiences, that's aware of our awareness of our experiences. While often invisible to us, this aspect of us can witness our experiences with openness, curiosity, calmness, and compassion—without an agenda and without getting entangled in the upsets or otherwise harmed by them in any way. If it's helpful, you might think of your Light as the "bigger you" that's aware of the "smaller you" that's entangled in upsets.

Learning to witness, through the eyes of your Light, the upsets and the experiences that precipitated the upsets is the fundamental shift in perspective that allows you to relate differently—and more productively—to your difficult thoughts and feelings. Psychiatrist Arthur Deikman argues that by dis-identifying from the thoughts and emotions that cause our emotional stress, "we lessen their impact and provide free space in which to choose an appropriate response." He says that by identifying with this aspect of us, "we can make a more realistic assessment of ourselves and our situation, permitting more effective and creative behavior."[8]

Put differently, if your Light is aware of upsets, you are by definition different from your upsets; if A observes B, A cannot equal B. If so, you can let go of the urge to purge your uncomfortable thoughts and feelings, because they no longer define the whole of who you are. You can witness your internal drama from a safe place without becoming overwhelmed by it. Your uncomfortable experiences still may be intense, but they are not the whole of you, they cannot hurt you, and they need not consume you.

Finally, from the perspective of your Light, you don't think to yourself, "I am my upsets," but, rather, think, "I am here, and *the* upsets are over there." Indeed, you might say to yourself, "There are the upsets." (Note the use of language: they are not *your* upsets.) Indeed, you can learn to see this aspect of yourself—this part of your mind that notices whatever you are noticing—in a radically new and helpful way: as a sanctuary, a tranquil and unchanging space from where you can hold all the upsets in awareness and just let them be without being harmed by them.

Jon Kabat-Zinn, in one of his recorded meditations, lyrically describes this sanctuary:

> Pure awareness [is] like the sky that can hold anything and everything—any aspect of our experience unfolding, including our darkest and most persistent and aversive thoughts and deepest fears, and yet is not tainted or disturbed or harmed by any of it. An awareness that sees and knows it all, just as it is. And in the seeing and in the knowing is free from the pull of negativity and habit, and provides a new place to reside, a new way to be and to live, that is trustworthy, authentic, and reconnects us to our intrinsic

wholeness, wisdom, and happiness. Fully embodied, at home right here, right now, in our own skin, with things exactly as they are.[9]

EXPERIENCING YOUR LIGHT

At this point, your head may still be spinning, so let's pause and return to earth. For starters, you might take a break to let some of these unfamiliar ideas sink in, or simply turn your mind to something else. When you are ready, you can learn more about the main ideas by trying several more experiential exercises. Feel free to pick and choose among them.

I have used the following exercise, "Noticing That You Are Noticing," which has its roots in acceptance and commitment therapy, with many leaders, who have found it quite helpful.[10] I suggest you go through this exercise slowly, pausing between the instructions.

D

NOTICING THAT YOU ARE NOTICING
(10–15 minutes)

Take a moment to get ready, and when you are—

- Notice your breath. Be aware that you are noticing your breath.

- Notice your thoughts. Be aware that you are noticing your thoughts.

- Notice what you can hear. Be aware that you are noticing what you can hear.

- Notice any stress that you might be experiencing. Be aware that you are noticing stress.

- Notice any sensations in your body. Be aware that you are noticing bodily sensations.

- Notice any upsets you might be experiencing. Be aware that you are noticing upsets.

So there's a part of your mind that notices everything. Over there are your experiences, and here you are noticing. What's more, the aspect of you that notices everything is not altered by what it notices; it is just aware. For example, the aspect of you that notices your stress is not stressed; it is just aware of your stress. The aspect of you that notices your upsets is not upset; it is just aware of your upsets.

As I described earlier, this aspect that can notice your experiences, separate from them, and not be altered by them is what I call your Light. Your Light is like the sky—bright and vast. And your experiences are like the weather. No matter how severe the weather, the sky has room for it. Even if your internal weather is like a hurricane, the sky is big enough to hold it—and not be altered by it. And like hurricanes, your internal storms come and go.

By viewing your experiences through the eyes of your Light, you are better able to separate from upsets and just be with them as they come and go. You are spacious enough to make room for all your small stuff instead of being swept away by it. *Here* you are; *there* are your upsets. Strange as it may sound, you need not be upset by your upsets.

Finally, thank your body and mind for its hard work, open your eyes, and return your attention to the day ahead with the intention of bringing your Light into your daily dealings.

The following exercise, "Making Space for Hands," is a continuation of the "Blinded by Hands" exercise. In this exercise, you'll use your hands to illuminate what disentanglement looks—and feels—like, and why it is important. To provide context for this exercise, I repeat the earlier exercise, adding the new material at the end of the exercise.

MAKING SPACE FOR HANDS   *(3–5 minutes)*

Start by doing two things: First, imagine you are at a meeting of your top staff—for example, a school district's academic cabinet, which consists of the chairs of various academic departments and the district's chief administrative officers. Second, imagine that your hands contain all your difficult thoughts, emotions, and memories—all the heavy stuff that you keep stewing over and that keeps you awake at night.

Now, slowly bring your hands up toward your face, with the palms together and facing you, until your hands cover your eyes. Now that you are blinded by your hands, blinded by all your heavy stuff, ponder these questions: Am I aware of what's happening in the academic cabinet meeting? Do I feel connected to my colleagues around me? Can I do those things I value—for example, interact with my colleagues, concentrate on the district's budget, exercise leadership? Notice that when you are totally entangled in your heavy stuff, you miss out on a lot. Your attention is not on the meeting. You are disconnected from the world around you. You cannot do those things that maximize your performance. You forget about the things that matter most to you.

Now, slowly lower your hands from your face, increasing the space between you and your heavy stuff. Notice as your hands no longer cover your eyes, you gain perspective on the room around you. You are no longer distracted or disconnected from your colleagues. You are fully present and able to do what you want to do. Notice that your hands are still there and your upsets have not gone away, but they no longer interfere with what you want to do.

When you are ready, slowly bring your attention back to the room and return to your day ahead.

D

To help you disentangle yourself from the contents of your mind, the following exercise, "Mets Parade," uses the metaphor of a passing parade to show how you can separate yourself from your thoughts and just watch them come and go.[11] These thoughts might be self-evaluations, the focus so far, but they could also be any thoughts your mind produces—for example, rules about what you can and cannot do, intrusive memories, judgments of others, and so on.

METS PARADE *(5–10 minutes)*

Imagine that the long-suffering New York Mets have finally won the World Series after their devastating loss in 2015— and a day has been set aside for a parade in the team's honor. On this brisk fall day, imagine you are watching the parade go by—giddy ballplayers in outsized convertibles, chirpy politicians hugging toddlers, and raucous high school bands losing the beat, all interspersed with gigantic floats, each with a smiling queen on a throne. Imagine for a moment just being there on the sidewalk, taking it all in—the sound of an approaching fife and drum corps, the sight of the Big Apple's bigwigs, food-cart aromas, the tang of a hot chili dog, and the clumsy touch of a neophyte pickpocket.

Now, imagine turning your attention to what's going on inside you—your moods, emotions, thoughts, and sensations (that is, your internal METS). Notice what's happening in your mind and body. Also, name your METS, each of which can be pleasant, difficult, or neutral. For example, you might say to yourself, "I'm in a bad mood because my two oldest kids couldn't come," or "I'm angry at the rowdy crowd," or "I should be back in the office going over my faculty evaluations." You might think, "I'm remembering marching in a band down Fifth Avenue when I was a kid," or "I'm beginning to freeze standing still behind the crowd fence," or even "I'm thinking this exercise is ridiculous!"

As your METS—moods, emotions, thoughts, and sensations—come to mind, notice them, name them, and imagine gently placing each of your METS, one at a time, on a different float in the parade as, one by one, the float comes into sight. Start by noticing the first float, and keep your eye on it as it comes closer to you. Then watch it as it passes in front of you and moves down the block carrying one of your METS with it. Continue placing each of your METS on a separate float—and just watch as each comes closer, passes you by, and then slowly disappears, carrying the contents of your mind out of sight.

When you are ready, slowly bring your attention back to the room, gently open your eyes, and return to the day ahead with the intention of stepping back and watching the parade of thoughts and emotions that pass by you, the observer.

D

ACCESSING YOUR LIGHT

In leadership settings, there are several practical ways to separate yourself from your upsets and to access your Light. A particularly powerful approach is through careful attention to the language you use in your self-talk—that is, the conversations you have with yourself, your internal dialogue. The importance of self-talk is well illustrated in the following exercise, "Self-Talk Matters," which is adapted from the work of Ann Weiser Cornell, a trailblazer in focusing.[12]

When we talk to ourselves about our upsets, the language we use can really matter because, as we have seen, it is so easy to get caught up with our heavy stuff and completely identify with it. When that happens, we disengage from the present moment and lose our perspective on what's happening in our lives. We undermine our clarity, our calmness, and our ability to perform at an optimal level.

SELF-TALK MATTERS *(5–10 minutes)*

I invite you to identify a difficult emotion that you are experiencing right now or have recently felt. For example, it could be frustration with the teachers union, regret about a new curriculum gone awry, sadness at the transfer of the school's best teacher, or boredom at the faculty meetings. It need not be the most difficult feeling you have recently experienced, but it should be one that has been on your mind.

Now, "say" your emotion to yourself like this: "I am —— [fill in the blank]." For example, you might say, "I am frustrated," "I am regretful," or "I am sad." (If you prefer, instead of saying "I am ——," you might say, "I feel ——." For example, "I feel frustrated," "I feel regretful.")

Next, take a moment to sit with your three-word sentence, and notice if anything happens inside of you—additional feelings, body sensations, thoughts. Notice if your sentence leads to others. For example, "I am angry" might lead to "I am a frustrated person," which might lead to "I'm unfit to be a leader." Pause for a moment, and see what you notice.

Now, make a small change in the language of your sentence. Instead of saying, "I am ——," say, "Something in me is ——." For example, "I am frustrated" becomes "Something in me is frustrated." When you are ready, try this shift in language with your emotion. Pause for a moment, and notice if you can feel a difference with this new self-talk, perhaps a difference in how your body holds your difficult emotion.

One last step: Add two more words to your sentence. Instead of saying, "Something in me is ——," say, "I notice something in me is ——." For example, "Something in me is frustrated" becomes "I notice something in me is frustrated."

Again, pause and notice if this tiny shift in self-talk makes a difference for you in how you carry the emotion. See if you feel the difference between saying "I'm frustrated" and saying "I notice something in me is frustrated."

When you are ready, open your eyes and return to the day ahead with the intention of using this new language when you experience upsets.

In other words, a good way to access your Light is by learning to step back psychologically from your upsets, notice that you are noticing them, and name the upsets you are noticing in the moment. In doing so, your self-talk illuminates the difference between Entangled Mind and your Light. It is the difference between silently saying "I'm furious at my boss" and "I notice something in me that's furious at my boss." Or between "I'm a failure as a leader" and "I sense something in me that feels like a failure as a leader." At first blush, these changes in self-talk may seem convoluted and awkward, but they can help you differentiate your Light from your thoughts and feelings.

Moreover, in a disquieting situation, if Entangled Mind were to ask the question "Who am I?," the answer, as we've seen, would probably be some version of this: "I *am* my upsetting thoughts, feelings, and sensations." Viewing the world through the lens of Entangled Mind, we identify with our upsets and react automatically, with little conscious control. In contrast, our Light's answer would probably be something like this: "I am that aspect of me that can make space for upsets and just let them be. I *am* much more than the upsets."

BENEFITS OF DISENTANGLING

This fundamental shift in perspective takes practice to develop. But it's worth the effort because it allows you to relate differently—and more productively—to your troubled parts. By identifying with your Light and remembering to make it your home base, you no longer feel a desperate need to escape difficulties—or overreact—because your uncomfortable thoughts and feelings no longer define "who I am." Your internal struggles may still be intense, but you can witness them from a safe place without becoming overwhelmed or hurt. No longer the whole of who you are, your upsets need not consume you nor control your actions. Instead of being your upsets, by identifying with your Light, you can be with your upsets as a nonjudgmental observer, making space for them to come and go. (In chapter 3, I briefly introduced focusing and internal family systems. Although both systems offer wise ways of being with your upsets, they go beyond the scope of this book.)

"It's very empowering to realize that it is totally up to us how we relate to the situation," says Joseph Goldstein. "Nobody makes us relate to our own emotions or the external situation in a particular way. Conditions may arise that bring up anger or fear, but how we relate to them is totally up to us. That's the great gift of the practice—we learn how to relate to the difficulties with a freer mind."[13]

Disentangling from upsets, then, has important practical consequences for leadership. By disrupting downward spirals caused by excessive identification and rumination, not to mention resistance and self-rebuke, you can *have* painful thoughts rather than be *had* by them, you can keep your attention on the leadership tasks at hand, and you can choose how you respond to disturbing events.

John Teasdale and colleagues make a similar point: "[We can] experience thoughts as part of the flow of life—in just the same way we experience sensations, sounds, feelings, and sights. We cultivate the ability to experience thoughts as *thoughts*—as mental events that enter and leave the mind. With this shift we rob thoughts of their power to upset us or control our actions. When we see thoughts for what they are—just thoughts, nothing but passing mental events—we can experience a wonderful sense of freedom and ease."[14]

And Rick Hanson echoes the point eloquently: "Letting your mind be, simply observing your experiences, gives you relief and perspective, like stepping out of a movie screen and watching from twenty rows back . . . In the light of an accepting, non-reactive awareness, your negative thoughts and feelings can sometimes melt away like morning mists on a sunny day."[15]

To sum up, learning to disentangle from Entangled Mind and establish your Light as your new home base is well worth the effort. The process of stepping back—scooching over to make room—and shifting identity can fundamentally change your relationship with upsets, allowing you to stop being their slave and start handling them effectively. Indeed, learning to show up as your Light just might be the very wellspring of your capacity to flourish as a leader. I invite you to pause and fully take in India.Arie's words: "I am light, I am light."

D

Allow Unease

> I have accepted fear as a part of life—
> specifically the fear of change . . . I have
> gone ahead despite the pounding in the
> heart that says: turn back.
>
> —*Erica Jong*

In a Nutshell ...

What This Step Is

- The ability—and willingness—to *open up* to discomfort just as it is in the moment, making space for the experiences that life throws at you even when they are unwelcome

What This Step Helps You Do

- Stop being a slave to troubling emotions that can steal your time, sap your energy, and destabilize your life
- Redirect your time, energy, and attention to pursuing value-inspired action (VIA) by wisely embracing the reality of the moment
- Open the door to emotional balance, deliberate choice, judicious action, and the experience of delight

---

FIRST ENCOUNTERS

I remember well when I first came across the main idea explored in this chapter—the *acceptance* part of acceptance and commitment therapy.[1] Back then, I was decidedly not accepting of acceptance. First of all, it seemed unthinkable. I'm a problem solver—that's what drew me into leadership work. I was motivated by trying to do my part in fixing the world, particularly for poor children ill served by our schools. Accept things the way they are? Not on your life.

Moreover, the notion of acceptance was scary too. In fact, having grown up as an adherent of Murphy's Law, I considered it downright dangerous. The idea of accepting my fears and doubts and confusion as a leader felt like jumping headfirst into a bottomless pit with no way to claw my way out. I'd spent a good part of my life resisting the pain that life brings. I knew it would take a lot of convincing—and personal experience—to start down what felt like a dangerous new path.

As things have turned out, I was dead wrong (as I've been with a lot of things in life). Partly I misunderstood the word *acceptance*, a clunky word that's easy to misunderstand, which is why I mainly use the word *allowing* instead, which is a little better. You can allow your internal pain while working as hard as you can to change the external world. To be sure, this chapter is not about submission and inaction in the face of injustice.

I've also learned that it's not dangerous to allow my pain to be as it is; it's certainly not pleasant, but it isn't about to kill me or cause me harm. I've also come to understand that to disallow my inner struggles is to deny a big part of who I am. Most important, allowing my stuff has opened doors to a more vital and fulfilling life, a life that I had cut off from myself and others in the past. It has taken me a lifetime to begin to understand the power of allowing the pain that life brings; I hope you can learn about the deep benefits of allowing as well.

LOOKING BACK—AND FORWARD

To start, let's recap where we are: In the first step of MY DANCE, we focused on the centrality of doing what matters to you, thereby living a life inspired by your deeply held values. Next, we looked at how to handle internal upsets so you don't get distracted from, or prevent yourself from engaging in, values-inspired action. To this end, we explored two building blocks of mindfulness—being in the present moment and disentangling from upsets—and surveyed their many benefits.

In this chapter, we examine a third building block of mindfulness, *allowing*, which is the exact opposite of our natural tendency to "scratch our itch"—that is, the urge to control our internal upsets, which typically undermines our capacity to be effective both at work and at home. Counterintuitive as it may sound, *allowing* means learning to willingly accept our difficulties as perfectly OK, to allow them to be just as they are, and to bring them along on our personal and professional leadership journey. We learn to itch, without always scratching.

To get a taste of what lies ahead in this chapter, let's begin with an exercise that captures the high cost of doggedly resisting your internal upheavals—trying to escape them, instead of accepting them. "Pushing Hands Away" is an extension of an earlier exercise that used the hands metaphor to illustrate the problems with getting entangled in—and blinded by—all your difficult thoughts and feelings.[2]

A

PUSHING HANDS AWAY   *(3–5 minutes)*

Again, imagine that your hands contain all your difficult thoughts, feelings, and memories. But this time, imagine that you want to get rid of all this emotional stuff that keeps you awake at night. So, what do you do? Push both hands up, up,

---

and away from you as far as you can. Straighten your arms, and push as hard as you can.

While you're pushing your heavy stuff away, ponder these questions: Does it work? Can I get rid of my stuff? Am I distracted from what matters most to me in life? And what about my shoulders—aren't they getting tired? What if I keep doing this—won't I become exhausted?

OK, now relax and place your hands in your lap. Notice the difference. Notice how you are less tired—and less distracted. Feel how much easier it is to do the things that matter to you. Also, note that your heavy stuff has not disappeared. It is still with you, but you are responding to it differently. As a result, it has much less influence over you. You can do the things that you value without being undermined by all your heavy stuff.

When you are ready, slowly bring your attention back to the room and return to your day ahead with the intention of allowing your heavy thoughts and feelings to be just as they are.

This improbable step of allowing what life brings—not always scratching our itch—opens us to wisely living life as it is and to keeping our attention on what matters most to us. Psychologist Zindel Segal and his colleagues make this point nicely: "The best way to 'get somewhere' is not to try to get anywhere at all, but to open to the way things actually are in this moment; this direct perception and observation will show us new ways of navigating outside the 'box' of our habitual patterns of reacting, seeing, and thinking about things."[3]

In essence, allowing means *welcoming* your internal upsets as part of who you are, rather than trying to avoid them, fix them, or banish them. To welcome discomfort, you must be willing to fully experience it, which is different from wanting it. "You may not like the feelings, you may wish it could be another way," say psychologists Susan Orsillo and Lizabeth Roemer, "but you can be willing to experience whatever comes up in order to take a valued action."[4]

Allowing is a stance we take toward discomfort—the choice to embrace what you may have thought of as the enemy while letting go of your urge to fix it. Allowing entails making room for your internal struggles and shortcomings with compassion, greeting them with an open heart, and turning toward them with curiosity. The thirteenth-century Persian poet Rumi echoes these sentiments about a welcoming stance in his beautiful and well-known poem:

THE GUEST HOUSE

This being human is a guest house.
Every morning a new arrival.
A joy, a depression, a meanness,
some momentary awareness comes
as an unexpected visitor.
Welcome and entertain them all!
Even if they are a crowd of sorrows,
who violently sweep your house
empty of its furniture,
still, treat each guest honorably.
He may be clearing you out
for some new delight.
The dark thought, the shame, the malice.
Meet them at the door laughing and invite them in.
Be grateful for whatever comes.
because each has been sent
as a guide from beyond.[5]

To think of our emotions as welcome and wise guides from afar, as Rumi suggests, is the opposite of resisting them and locking them out.

To be sure, allowing is not the same as passivity or giving up. Nor does acceptance imply a begrudging attitude of resignation toward whatever you are accepting. If anything, this book is about following your dreams, even when the obstacles are high; it is decidedly not about teaching you to be a doormat. Indeed, you can allow what's happening here and now in your internal world *and* work to improve things in the external world. For example, you might say to yourself, "Right now, I'm feeling really discouraged about school reform. I'm going to acknowledge that feeling—and I'm going to do everything in my power to make schools a better place for kids."

Acceptance is not "nihilistic self-defeat," Steven Hayes and Spencer Smith say. "[N]either is it tolerating and putting up with your pain. It is very, very different than that. Those heavy, sad, dark forms of 'acceptance' are almost the exact opposite of the active, vital embrace of the moment that we mean."[6]

And acceptance of every single unwanted thought and emotion is not what is being advocated here. Rather, acceptance makes sense when it facilitates movement toward what matters most to you. Here's a metaphor that makes the point: Suppose you love mountain climbing and you are determined to climb one, far from home—a mountain that you've never seen before. When you arrive at the foot of the mountain, you discover that it's surrounded by a swamp. The only way to get to the mountain is to wade hip-high through the stagnant water, keeping a keen eye out for snakes. You hold your breath and slog through the swamp because climbing the mountain really matters to you.[7]

The core of allowing is illustrated by the familiar Chinese finger trap, where the goal is to free yourself after inserting your index fingers into each end of a woven bamboo tube. If you try to pull your fingers out straight and fast, the tube tightens. The more you struggle to escape, the more you are trapped. The paradox of the Chinese finger trap is a metaphor for freeing yourself to make choices by letting go of your internal drama. But this is just the opposite of what we have usually been taught.

The fundamental lesson about allowing is captured in the following exercise, "Picking Up the Boulder," which is based on a parable cited by psychologists Shauna L. Shapiro and Linda E. Carlson.[8] The story is about an unusual teacher walking with her students in the woods. Although the exercise takes only a few minutes, take as much time as you have to try it out in real life.

PICKING UP THE BOULDER *(3–5 minutes)*

Begin by slowly reading the following parable:

> "Students, do you see that boulder?" a teacher asks while walking with her students.
>
> "Yes, teacher, we see that boulder!" respond her students.
>
> "And is the boulder heavy?" asks the teacher.
>
> "Oh yes, very heavy," respond the students.
>
> "Not if you don't pick it up," replies the teacher.

Take a few moments now to savor this story and reflect on what it means to you. As you do so, consider this question: Can you learn to let troubling thoughts and feelings "just be," by leaving them alone and not picking them up? Even though upsets may be painful, can you use your skills to *not* make them heavier in the moment?

As an experiment, try this approach the next time you are on a distressingly long, slow line in the school cafeteria, or get stuck in a traffic jam on the way to work, or encounter a pet peeve with your board of trustees and find your emotions building up into a big boulder. Can you notice your big boulder, your agitation, and your impulse to act; make room for your feelings; and choose not to pick up the boulder?

A

When you are ready, return to the day ahead with the intention of testing this approach the next time you run into a big boulder in your internal life.

MY DANCE helps you learn both to be fully present and to disentangle from your upsets. As we are learning in this chapter, it also helps you accept your here-and-now discomfort for what it is—a normal part of living, learning, and leading—and allow it to be just as it is. You learn to pause and let go of your urge to jettison discomfort and to calmly consider more effective alternatives. You learn to go with the flow of your feelings in the moment, while working like mad to change what can be changed in your outer world.

ACCEPTING ACCEPTANCE

This step of MY DANCE often generates skepticism among leaders, at least in my experience. After all, the notion of acceptance is so contrary to what seems like the right thing to do that it's hard to fully understand—and an even harder idea to accept! Acceptance can feel like giving up the good fight or not being tough enough to lick the problems we face. It can also be scary to think about the consequences of accepting such feelings as intense regret, frustration, or disappointment.

In assessing the value of acceptance, we do well to compare this strategy for dealing with difficulties with the alternative: resisting our struggles and trying to control them. Below, two exercises and a story about monkeys make this comparison. These examples should illustrate the futility and high cost of resistance strategies in dealing with the present moment. After these three, I invite you to consider several additional exercises meant to help you experience acceptance—and practice developing the skill of allowing.

I hope these learning tools dampen your skepticism about this seemingly crazy idea and trigger your willingness to give this approach a try. Remember that acceptance can help you do what matters most to you as a leader, an educator, and a human being.

To start, compare *acceptance* with three other common responses to upsets. The visualization exercise "Handling Wild Horses" uses the imagery of these animals to capture both the intense energy of emotions and the natural inclination to escape intense feelings.

HANDLING WILD HORSES   *(5–10 minutes)*

Imagine standing inside a grassy corral that's attached to a rickety old barn. Further, imagine half a dozen wild horses in the corral. In your mind's eye, watch the horses, and observe their movements. Sometimes, the horses quietly roam around, stopping to chew the grass. Other times, they're frisky, prancing about and throwing their heads. And lots of times, these powerful animals are extremely agitated—downright frightening as they buck and snort and gallop and threaten to jump the fence.

Now, imagine that your emotions are like these wild horses: sometimes quiet, other times frisky, and lots of the time really acting up. In this exercise, contemplate four ways to handle your emotions—your very own wild horses—particularly when they become powerful and agitated, when it feels as if they're galloping all around you and inside your head. By *handle*, I mean finding the best way for you to interact with your wild horses.

First, you can respond to being surrounded by wild horses by *jumping the fence and running for cover.* After all, it's only human to avoid being trampled. What's more, this response does provide short-term relief—a feeling of safety. But ponder this question: In the long term, can you run away every time your emotions become powerful and

A

upsetting? Won't you miss out on a lot of life if you always try to escape your feelings?

Second, you can respond to your wild horses by *locking them in the barn*. In the short term, that should work—even though they'll crash about and try to kick the door down. But in the long term, can you lock up your powerful emotions, or will they someday break free and race back, bucking even stronger?

Third, you can respond to your wild horses by *forcing them to submit*. Indeed, you might start by putting a bridle on the strongest stallion and trying to ride him until he quiets down. Now, that might seem brave, but consider this question: can you always ride your emotions until they submit to your control? How long can you keep this up? Or might this just make your wild horses even wilder?

Finally, consider a different response, one that doesn't try to control your wild horses, leave you at their mercy, or have you run away from them. Instead, imagine stepping back from the fray, watching your wild horses, and allowing them to be just as they are without interference, without judgment. Imagine giving them the space and time to release their nervous energy inside the corral.

Now, this fourth way to respond to your wild horses may feel risky in the short term, but consider these five questions:

- If you step back and just observe your wild horses, might not you feel safe enough to stay with them without running away?
- Couldn't you stay with them without locking them up?
- Could you stay with them without trying to subdue them?
- Further, if you give your wild horses room to gallop, might they not quiet down of their own accord?
- And finally, if you stay with your wild horses just as they are, might not you learn to handle them, even when they are at their wildest?

Consider the four ways of responding to your wild horses. The first three are aimed at controlling or avoiding your strong emotions. Do any of these approaches sound familiar? If so, do your attempts to control your emotions really work in the long term? If these three responses don't work, might you be willing to consider the final approach—allowing things to be as they are? Are you willing to try this counter-intuitive approach and see if it works for you?

Finally, thank your vivid imagination for all its hard work, open your eyes, take a quick stretch, and return to your day ahead with the intention of turning what you have learned into action.

This wild-horses exercise illustrates the power of allowing, but what exactly do you do with your troubling emotions when they're not front and center in your mind? You can bring your upsets with you as you pursue your values, as illustrated in the next exercise, "Toting Your Upsets." The exercise, which also calls on your imagination, can be done alone or in a group, where you can compare your own reactions with others'.

A

TOTING YOUR UPSETS   *(5–10 minutes)*

Begin by spotlighting all the heavy stuff that's been bugging you over the last couple of months or so, putting aside for the moment all the good things in your life. Bring to mind things like intrusive memories, distressing emotions, gloomy thoughts, uncomfortable body sensations, intense urges to act—all the stuff that perhaps you keep rehashing in your mind.

Now imagine sitting at your office desk and writing out on separate sheets of paper each thought or emotion that's getting under your skin, causing you anguish. For example, memories of not getting promoted to school principal or deep regret for making a stupid decision about a student fight. They could be troubling questions like "Should I quit? What's with the tightness in my throat? Should I tell my superintendent to take a hike?"

When you are ready, imagine turning to the shelves of books behind your desk and putting each of these sheets of paper into a separate book; like the books, your upsets can be pretty heavy. One by one, you insert your upsets into the books—and put all of the books on your desk. Finally, you decide to gather these books into a tote bag to get rid of them. You're not surprised to see how easy it is to fill the bag to the top.

So, what do you do now with your tote bag filled with heavy stuff? Well, you first try to shove it under your desk, but then you can no longer push your chair into the spot. You try to hide the bag in the closet, but you trip over it whenever you go for supplies. Getting a bit exasperated, you then decide to push it away from you as far as you can, on the top shelf of your bookcase, but pretty soon you're exhausted by the effort and you notice you're not getting any work done. Try as you might, you can't get rid of the bag. So, you say to yourself, "You know what; I'll just take my bag of heavy stuff with me wherever I go—after all, it's part of who I am."

That afternoon, you have an important meeting across town. You grab your tote bag and take it with you on the subway to the meeting. After a successful meeting, back home with you goes your tote bag.

That evening, you mull over your experiences with your bag full of heavy stuff. You ask yourself, "What is to be learned from this exercise?" You come up with four takeaways:

- I need to stop trying to control those things I cannot control—and that includes my emotions; it just makes things worse.

- I waste a ton of hours and oomph trying to escape my inescapable heavy stuff; I have better things to do with my life.
- I need to work on controlling the things I can control—and that includes my attention, my actions, and the expression of my emotions.
- I don't need to first free myself from my heavy stuff before I turn to what matters to me; I can start going for the gold right now.

In a word, I can act on what I value and also bring along with me all my heavy stuff.

The point that acceptance is often the best choice—or more realistically, the least bad option for moving forward—is also nicely made by Susan Pollak and her colleagues in their retelling of an amusing tale, which I've slightly embellished:

> When the British colonized India, many of the expatriates were homesick and badly missed being able to play golf. So, an enterprising group of imperial civil servants set about constructing a golf course on the outskirts of Delhi. A problem arose, however, when the local monkeys joined in the game, creating havoc by throwing the little white balls wherever they liked.
>
> The frustrated golfers were used to getting their way, so they formed a committee with the task of fixing the monkey problem. First they decided to build a high fence around the golf course. But the monkeys delighted in climbing over it. The committee then decided to round up the monkeys and cart them away. But the monkeys returned.
>
> At their wits' end, the committee members held an emergency meeting. After a long and fruitless discussion of

various options and on the verge of seeing the group disband in despair, a quiet golfer in the corner piped up: "What if we just play the ball where the monkey drops it?"[9]

Isn't much of life like playing the ball where the monkey drops it, instead of working ourselves into a sweat about things we can't control? Indeed, at the heart of acceptance is allowing difficult stuff to be as it is.

The wisdom of allowing what's beyond our control is strikingly captured in the following poem by Danna Faulds:

ALLOW

There is no controlling life.
Try corralling a lightning bolt,
containing a tornado. Dam a
stream, and it will create a new
channel. Resist, and the tide
will sweep you off your feet.
Allow, and grace will carry
you to higher ground. The only
safety lies in letting it all in—
the wild with the weak; fear,
fantasies, failures and success.

When loss rips off the doors of
the heart, or sadness veils your
vision with despair, practice
becomes simply bearing the truth.
In the choice to let go of your
known way of being, the whole
world is revealed to your new eyes.[10]
DANNA FAULDS

So, are you less skeptical—and more ready—to accept acceptance as an important skill? If so, the next exercise, "Allowing Intense Emotions," can help you experience what allowing feels like. In particular, note how the exercise includes elements of step 3 of MY DANCE (disentangling and your Light), which goes hand-in-hand with acceptance, and helps you willingly allow intense feelings that otherwise might be unbearable. This exercise is adapted from the work of acceptance and commitment therapy specialist Russ Harris.[11]

ALLOWING INTENSE EMOTIONS
(15–20 minutes)

Please go through this exercise slowly, pausing between sentences. Take a moment to get yourself ready for a look inside. By this time, you may have developed a personal routine that you follow to become more grounded, present, and aware.

When you are ready, identify a painful emotion in your work life right now. Examples might be anger at a colleague for an insulting comment, anxiety over chairing an upcoming meeting, sadness over a pet project that just got axed, or humiliation over a tactless quote from you in the school newspaper. The painful issue should be something you feel intensely about—indeed, enough that you're inclined to take steps to escape or avoid the feeling. But the feeling cannot be so intense that you recoil from the idea of even exploring it in this exercise.

Having identified an intense emotion, observe its manifestations within you. In particular, take a moment to scan your body for sensations. You might experience these sensations in your stomach, your neck, your chest, or elsewhere. And

A

then zoom in on the part of your body where you're experiencing this emotion most intensely.

Now notice the feeling as if you were a curious scientist encountering the emotion for the first time. Observe its characteristics—for example, is it big or small, hot or cold, tight or loose, light or heavy, throbbing or still? When your mind wanders, thank your mind, and bring your attention back to your body, back to this exploration of the intense feeling.

As you observe this physical manifestation of your feeling, notice that you are noticing it, and acknowledge the presence of your Light. From this seat of awareness, this broad perspective, make space for your feeling to be just as it is. Breathe into it. Make room for it. Be with your intense feeling; don't try to fix it.

You may not want it or like it, and that's OK. You may feel a strong urge to push it away or run away from it. If so, acknowledge the urge, and don't act on it. Continue to notice and make room for it. Don't try to get rid of it or fix it.

As you notice your intense feeling, remember that your emotions are your friend. They provide you with helpful information. They tell you that you care. They tell you that there are things in life that matter to you. They tell you that you are a normal human being. Remember, resisting your emotions and trying to get rid of them is to diminish part of what makes you human.

When you are ready, slowly bring your attention back to the room, open your eyes, and carry this open sense of acceptance with you throughout the day.

Over time, you might choose to repeat this exercise with different emotions to renew your experience of acceptance. If you do this exercise more than once, you might experiment with increasing the intensity of the emotions you accept.

Throughout this chapter, we've explored the value of allowing, mainly as it compares with the alternative of resistance. We've seen that acceptance has far fewer costs; it may be scary, but it won't hurt you (unlike resistance, which can backfire in the long run). But it's also important to emphasize the positive benefits of acceptance. For one, it opens you up to your emotions, which are an integral part of being a whole human being and which are important sources of information about what's happening in your world as a professional in the field of education.

Another positive benefit of acceptance: it can be a truly liberating experience, freeing the time and energy misspent on trying to control your upsets and keep them at bay. Moreover, acceptance enormously expands your choices in life because you no longer are running from this, hiding from that, and avoiding whatever gives you discomfort. And most important, acceptance clears the path to pursue with newfound vigor the things that matter most to you. For all these reasons, Russ Harris, reflecting on his many years as a leading trainer in acceptance and commitment therapy, concludes that "the single most important lesson I've learned . . . is the wisdom of dropping the struggle with discomfort."[12]

TAKING STOCK

At this point, you might want to pause and take a break. After all, in quick order I've placed on your plate several rich and difficult-to-digest morsels. In particular, the notion of acceptance is a radical idea whose merit may take time for you to evaluate and absorb. You need time to decide whether acceptance works for you.

"I Can't Believe It!," the final exercise in this chapter, helps you take stock of where you are and recaps, in perhaps an amusing way, both the skills you are beginning to develop and the benefits they offer. It highlights a thank-god-it's-not-me predicament of a college president in an airplane ride from hell, where no good options exist. Again, the exercise taps into the potential power—and humor—of drawing on our vivid imaginations.[13]

I CAN'T BELIEVE IT!   (5–10 minutes)

Imagine you're a college president from New York visiting San Francisco with your family on spring break. Late in the day, you receive an urgent call from your deputy about a newspaper article alleging serious wrongdoings at your college in the recruitment of athletes. Your heart begins to race as you listen to the disturbing details. Worried about the mess blowing up, you decide to fly home immediately to size up the situation firsthand, deal with this potential crisis, and hold a press conference tomorrow at noon to update the community.

Last to board a red-eye flight to JFK Airport, you notice that the plane is full, except for the two seats next to you. "What great luck," you tell yourself. "I can quietly think through my strategy and then stretch out to get some shut-eye." Just as the cabin door is being closed, a breathless young couple rushes on board carrying a screaming baby. As they head for the seats next to you, you think to yourself, "Holy moly, I cannot believe this is happening to me!"

As the plane ascends to cruising altitude, the couple tries everything to soothe their baby boy, but he just keeps screeching. Meanwhile, your mind is spinning over how you got into this mess. You worry about being exhausted at the press conference and rebuke yourself for forgetting your noise-canceling earphones. Sitting there, you begin to obsess over how to escape this unbearable situation so you can be fresh, focused, and prepared tomorrow.

So, what are your options here? You can spend the next five hours sulking. Or you can bury your feelings and join the couple in their vain efforts to pacify their son. Neither option will make things better, you conclude, so you dash to the toilet to think—and hide. After ten minutes, a flight attendant knocks on the door, asking you to return to your seat.

As you slowly walk back down the aisle—feeling exasperated, but not knowing what to do—you suddenly recall the seven steps of MY DANCE, which you had learned at a Harvard workshop. Four steps stand out:

You recall your commitment to step 1: *mind your values*. This step triggers your memory of what's really important to you, which includes being well prepared. So you commit to getting some work done when you return to your seat. You also remember that being a good listener matters to you. So you say to yourself, "When I sit down, I'll try to hear the family's perspective. Mom and Dad must be distraught—and the baby in a lot of pain."

You recall step 2: *yield to now*. So you stop and decide to take a full minute to focus on your breath, slowly breathing in and breathing out, to get grounded and centered. You hope this will calm you down a bit, anchor you in the present moment, and take your mind off the imbroglio back home and the worrisome press conference.

You recall step 3: *disentangle from upsets*. So you take a minute to step back and just watch your racing mind as it spews out one wild worry after another. In that moment, you gain some perspective, which allows you to watch your troubling thoughts and feelings without taking them all so personally and twisting yourself into a pretzel.

You recall step 4: *allow unease*. "Well," you say to yourself, "this is the hardest skill, but it sure beats the alternatives—spending the whole flight resisting reality, fretting about the pickle I'm in, and beating myself up for forgetting my earphones."

So you decide to give all these new skills a try. When you finally get back to your seat, you engage the couple in a

A

conversation. Mostly, you listen and play back their words so they understand that you understand—and care. After a few minutes, they politely end the conversation to soothe their son.

Then, you focus your attention on your notes and plans for tomorrow. You certainly don't want the screaming, but there it is—a baby in pain doing what babies do. You decide to allow the sound to be just as it is and focus on your work. A minute or two later, however, your mind pipes up and says, "This is ridiculous; I can't put up with this noise." When this happens, you step back and notice this thought and bring your mind back to allowing the pain and unease that life brings, which makes it possible for you to concentrate on your preparation.

Eventually you doze off—only to be awakened a few hours later as the wheels are lowered. As you prepare to exit the plane, you help the couple with their luggage—and wish them well with their still-crying son. Later that day, at the press conference, you impress the reporters with your grasp of the situation, your calm, your presence, and your clarity.

Back at the office later that afternoon, you call your husband.

"How was the press conference?" he asks.

"Well," you reply, "I was exhausted, but never have I felt more focused and effective. I demonstrated that we're on top of the situation. I'll give you the details when I get back home tonight."

"Great," he responds, and then adds, "I hate red-eye flights—how was yours?"

You pause for a moment and say, "Actually, it was an amazing flight. I found within me the capacity to step back and accept what normally would drive me nuts. I also was able to act from the values I stand for—and stay in the moment. Rarely have I felt more fully empowered, more fully alive, more effective."

Just then, your assistant reminds you of your staff meeting on the allegations about athletes. You say good-bye, grab your files, and head toward the conference room. As you stride down the hall, with a spring in your step, you take justifiable pride in how you've handled the plane trip—and the would-be crisis—so far.

Like the college president in this story, with practice you too can learn to apply these first four steps of MY DANCE, even in unusually stressful circumstances. When you are ready, in the next chapter, we'll move away from mindfulness skills in the service of values-inspired action (presence, disentangling, and acceptance) toward a complementary spotlight on nourishing ourselves.

A

CHAPTER NINE

Nourish Yourself

To keep a lamp burning, we have to keep putting oil in it.

—*Mother Teresa*

In a Nutshell ...

What This Step Is

- The ability to make room for *everyday activities* that can renew your body, your mind, your heart, and your spirits in the face of a stress-filled life

What This Step Helps You Do

- Replenish your energy, restore your perspective, revitalize your sense of well-being, and ensure your resilience

- Nip in the bud the downward spirals of unhelpful thoughts and feelings that are often triggered by moments of stress

- Flourish as a leader in difficult times by countering the brain's tendency to be Velcro for the negative and Teflon for the positive

---

SANTA CLAUS

While I was dean, every December I picked a day to dress up as Santa Claus. With the help of my resourceful assistant, we rented a costume, belted a pillow around my waist, and powdered my cheeks and nose with rouge. In full regalia, I spent several hours crisscrossing Appian Way and walking the halls of the Harvard Ed School, jingling my sleigh bells and chanting ho ho ho. And along the way, I visited every office, offering season's greetings and handing out candy canes. In return, I got looks of bemused surprise and lots of chuckles.

Why, you might ask, did I do such a nutty thing? Well, back then, I would have said that playing Santa Claus was a way to help reduce the end-of-semester tension widespread across campus; it was my way of caring for the community at a particularly stressful time of year.

True enough, my colleagues confirmed that my antics helped humanize a high-pressure place. But now looking back, I realize that I was also playing Santa Claus to help *myself*. At that time of year, I was regularly exhausted, wrung out by the pace at Harvard, and feeling a bit overwhelmed. Somehow, I intuitively knew I needed to have some fun. I needed to engage in self-care. I needed to nourish myself. And somehow I knew that this was not an act of self-indulgence, but what I needed to do to continue to serve the school.

I start with this story because almost all of the educators I know are exceptionally decent and caring people. And yet they care for themselves last, if at all. Many believe they should be martyrs for the cause. Here I invite you to embrace—for your own well-being and for the well-being of your organization—a new golden rule: Do unto yourself as you would do unto others. For if you do not nourish yourself, you cannot nourish others. Here I offer a collection of practical ways to take care of yourself so you can better achieve your dreams of helping others— dreams that brought you to work as an educator.

LOOKING BACK—AND FORWARD

In different ways, all seven steps of MY DANCE nourish the mind, the heart, and the body. To live by your values, to be fully present in the moment, to step back and gain perspective on your troubling thoughts and feelings, to allow wholeheartedly what life places on your doorstep—all of these practices sustain us as we encounter the pitfalls and pleasures of leadership work. If you add self-compassion to the mix (to be discussed in chapter 10), you have a solid foundation for self-care.

In this chapter, I spotlight everyday nourishing activities that both complement the focus on mindfulness and values-inspired action and match the online *Free Dictionary* definition of *nourish*: "supply with what is necessary for life, health, and growth." I hope to expand your repertoire of wholesome ways to care for yourself, to spark introspection about the balance of nourishing versus depleting activities in your life, and to encourage you to seek out nourishing activities, particularly when you are feeling overwhelmed and drained and when you are sure you don't have the time.[1]

I emphasize the word *wholesome* because some beneficial activities can be harmful when not used in moderation. Physical exercise, for example, can be damaging if taken to the extreme. Most important, self-care can be counterproductive if primarily used as a way to escape your troubling thoughts and feelings—for example, running away every time you experience conflict or stress.

N

Nourishing activities are quite important because what we actually do moment-to-moment at work can have a big impact on how well we feel and whether we flourish, not to mention its impact on our productivity. Psychologist Mark Williams and journalist Danny Penman describe the debilitating effects of what has been called the "exhaustion funnel." As the pressures grow, many of us spiral down through periods of sleep disturbance and fatigue, then unexplained physical symptoms and irritability, then joylessness and hopelessness, deep exhaustion, and, finally, burnout.[2]

"The funnel is created," say Williams and Penman, "as you narrow the circle of your life to focus on solving your immediate problems. As you spiral down the funnel, you progressively give up more and more of the enjoyable things in life (which you come to see as optional) to make way for the more 'important' things such as work. As you slide even further down, you give up even more of the things that nourish you, leaving yourself increasingly exhausted, indecisive and unhappy. You are eventually spat out at the bottom, a shadow of your former self."[3] Might this grim picture sound familiar to you?

Nourishing activities are also very important because they can act as a counterweight to what has been called the "negativity bias," as spelled out by neuropsychologist Rick Hanson in his compelling book, *Hardwiring Happiness*. Hanson starts with a crucial question: "Why is it easier to ruminate over hurt feelings than it is to bask in the warmth of feeling loved? Your brain was wired in such a way when it evolved, primed to learn quickly from bad experiences, but not so much from good ones. It's an ancient survival mechanism that turned the brain into Velcro for the negative, but Teflon for the positive."[4]

Hanson goes on to say, "Life isn't easy, and having a brain wired to take in the bad and ignore the good makes us worried, irritated, and stressed . . . This makes you come down harder on yourself than you do on other people, feel inadequate even when you get a hundred things done, and feel lonely even when support is all around you."[5]

So, what can you do to override the brain's negativity bias? What can you do to avoid the exhaustion funnel? How can you feel a little bit better when you are feeling beat and blue? Drawing on the research of the scientists cited above and others, as well as my own experiences, I present below several kinds of nourishment, along with numerous examples, ending with more from Hanson on how to "take in the good."[6]

I begin with "Self-Care Profile," an exercise that involves taking stock of what you do at work right now and looking at whether these activities either nourish or deplete you. It's a good place to start because what we actually do at work can have a big impact on how we feel. In doing the exercise, you might observe your behavior over a few days before you record your observations and reflections.

SELF-CARE PROFILE *(20–30 minutes)*

When you are ready, step back and carefully consider these three questions:

- Of the things I do day in, day out, which of them are nourishing—adding to my energy, serenity, pleasure, perspective, resilience?
- Which activities drain me—contribute to my being beat and blue?
- And what practical steps am I deliberately taking to increase nourishing activities and decrease depleting activities?

If answering these questions is particularly difficult for you, you might want to spend some extra time examining your daily activities to improve your self-awareness about your routine behavior.

Next, when you are ready, turn what you notice into two lists, one of nourishing activities and one of depleting activities. Making a list can help you see more clearly exactly what you are doing—and motivate you to rebalance your life in the direction of adding more nourishing activities.

N

To improve your capacity for self-care, here are three other things to remember. First, think small; you can get started—anywhere—taking one step at a time. Once you start small, you are likely to discover that you can find time in your busy schedule and that additional action steps will therefore be easier to implement.

Second, build these new activities into your daily schedule before you think you need them. Why? Because leaders often resist taking time out for themselves, especially when stress is high and spirits are low.

Finally, when you are feeling down, motivation usually follows action, not the reverse, so you need to nourish yourself even when you do not feel like doing so. John Teasdale and his colleagues nail the point this way: "What you do affects how you feel. Most important: *You can change how you feel by changing what you do* . . . You can turn activity into a simple yet powerful way to raise mood and enhance well-being . . . When you feel low spirits, drained, with all your energy going or gone, take your time to ask yourself: 'How can I best take care of myself right now?'"[7]

MAKING ROOM FOR R & R

It's easy to ignore what research indicates—namely, the importance of rest—getting close to seven to eight hours of sleep every night. Moreover, studies suggest the value of a short daily nap, a practice followed by leaders from John F. Kennedy to Winston Churchill.[8] Rest, in various forms, can boost energy, reduce grumpiness, sharpen concentration, and foster clearheaded decisions. At least, that's the way it works for me.

In her book Thrive, Arianna Huffington extolls the bedrock importance of getting ample sleep. She reviews the scientific evidence and recounts how the lack of sleep nearly wrecked her career—and life.[9] Closer to home, a psychiatrist friend, Brent Forester, recently told me that when people are tired, hungry, or sick, they are much more prone to overreact emotionally.

Deep relaxation is also important because, for too many of us, our home base is chronic stress. "We now know that well over 60 percent of visits to a doctor are stress-related," says the Benson-Henry Institute for Mind Body Medicine.[10] It's as if our fight-or-flight switch gets stuck in the on position and we are constantly on high alert. Hypervigilance is exhausting and bad for your health, but thankfully, there are a number of proven techniques to flip the switch and deeply relax.

Here's a word about the granddaddy of proven ways to elicit the *relaxation response*, a term coined some forty years ago by physician Herbert Benson at the Harvard Medical School.[11] In essence, Benson's method, spelled out in the following exercise, "Relaxation Response," involves sitting quietly, choosing a simple word or phrase to repeat to yourself (or an image to focus on), and concentrating all your attention on it for several minutes, returning to it each time you become aware that your mind has wandered. If you do this each day, Benson says, you can access a relaxed state with remarkable benefits for your work life. The benefits range from lower blood pressure to greater ease in dealing with important decisions.

N

RELAXATION RESPONSE *(12–15 minutes)*

Many approaches can trigger the relaxation response, but here is the standard eight-step sequence that has been used at the Harvard Medical School for decades.

- Pick a focus word, phrase, image, or short prayer. Or focus on your breathing, if that works for you.
- Find a quiet place, and sit calmly in a comfortable position.
- Close your eyes.
- Progressively relax all your muscles from your toes to the top of your head.

- Breathe slowly and naturally. As you exhale, repeat silently your word or phrase, or picture your image, or simply focus on your breathing rhythm.
- Assume a passive attitude. When thoughts intrude, say to yourself, "Oh well," and return to your focus.
- Continue with this exercise for about twelve to fifteen minutes.
- Practice this approach at least once daily.

You might ask how this exercise differs from mindfulness meditation. The answer is mainly in its intention—namely, to elicit physiological relaxation, rather than a focus on developing your concentration, awareness, or insight.

SAVORING EVERYDAY ACTIVITIES

Leaders in education usually feel like they're supposed to be task directed and single-mindedly focused only on work; after all, the challenges are so great, and the needs of students cry out for our attention. But if you don't make time for wholesome activities that give you a sense of pleasure and satisfaction, you increase your chances of burnout.

Doing Pleasurable Things

You might start by being kind to your body—for example, taking a long shower, sitting in the sun, occasionally eating your favorite dessert. And do things that you find particularly enjoyable, like listening to music, taking a bike ride, watching a movie, kayaking, stepping out to dance, or reading a mystery while lying in a hammock. Of course, it's important how you seek these pleasures—mindfully, instead of rushing about seeking one distraction after another.

In the pursuit of wholesome pleasure, every once in a while, I make time for a massage. My masseuse, Heidi Fischbach, not only soothes my body with her supple hands, bringing me relaxation and pleasure, but also touches my soul with her image-filled writings about self-care and living on earth, as I mentioned in chapter 7. In a recent blog, she wrote about the importance of feeling supported, which can go hand in hand with pleasure: "Well, feeling totally supported is like sitting in the queen of all chairs, a chair that truly has your back. The queen of all chairs makes even the question of support obsolete. It's a chair that you can plop every last bit of the good the bad and the ugly of yourself into without a thought—let alone a second thought—pertaining to support. That kind of chair."[12]

Do you have that kind of chair? A person, a place, an activity that makes you feel like you're sitting in the queen of all chairs? The kind of chair that provides support and comfort and pleasure?

Being present with your five senses is still another way to produce pleasant feelings that can nurture you. Like the "Five-Sense Pause," the exercise aimed at dealing with difficulties (see chapter 6), the following exercise, "Strolling to Your Senses," spotlights a relaxed stroll and is another good way to connect with your five senses. It can be used in any environment—here in the Boston area, I use a setting by the sea. But you might go for a five-sense stroll anywhere you want, perhaps in a quiet place near your office. What's more, you can do this exercise as an act of imagination. Take as long as you like, soaking in the sights and sounds.

N

STROLLING TO YOUR SENSES *(10–15 minutes)*

Close your eyes, and imagine taking a stroll by the sea. Or better yet, take an actual walk of your choice. In either case, instead of planning and fretting as we often do when we go for a walk, concentrate on all five of your senses, one sense by one. Pause as long as you like between senses. You might slowly describe to yourself what you are sensing:

- Now, I'm watching diving seabirds . . .
- Now, I'm smelling the salt air . . .
- Now, I'm hearing the sound of breaking waves . . .
- Now, I'm tasting brine on my lips . . .
- Now, I'm feeling the sand between my toes . . .

If your walk was imaginary, open your eyes when you feel ready, or if you took a real walk, return to your workplace. Greet the rest of the day with the intention of focusing your attention on concrete experiences that give you pleasure.

As the above exercise shows, sometimes the best way to nourish ourselves is just to be in contact with the reality of the moment, sense by sense. Here's a story that illustrates the power of being present with your five senses and the pleasure it can bring even under difficult circumstances. Imagine how this story could be adapted to match your own professional trials.

Recently, I shared a draft of this chapter with my sister Jean, a retired teacher who lives in Florida. Jean is going blind and lives alone in a tiny apartment near the ocean. She spends much of her time worrying about where she will live and how she will manage when she is completely blind. Here's an excerpt from the handwritten letter Jean wrote to me after reading a draft of this chapter:

No sleep at night. My mind is cluttered with chatter. I read your draft and felt a glimmer. The idea of "using the five senses" appealed to me and seemed easy enough to put into my super-stressed life.

I got into bed, took a deep breath, and cleared my mind as much as possible.

- *Hearing:* What is that sound? Realizing it was the crashing of waves, I could not believe this was a sound unknown to me here. I never listened before—too distraught. My god, this is music for my mind.
- *Feeling: What* do I feel, not *how* do I feel. Ummm. I moved my feet and found cool, soothing spots on my soft sheets. Nice, very nice.
- *Tasting:* Now into this exercise and more relaxed, I considered the inside of my mouth. (Who does this? Not me, ever, but it was interesting.) I experienced a mixture of toothpaste and garlic. Made me laugh.
- *Smelling:* I took a deep breath of air. What is that odor? I was smelling my Chihuahua cuddled next to me. Now, content. Happy. Drowsy.
- *Seeing:* I opened my eyes and saw white fur. My precious cat was a flower at my feet. I looked out the window; there was—yes!—a full moon for me.
- Every night, I look forward to this exercise. It transports me into a realm of appreciation and calmness. I can now be aware of the gifts surrounding me. My mind was unable to absorb anything but fear of the future. So, as the day ends and I seek sleep, I put my head on a new pillow that says Home Sweet Home.

All of us will encounter times when we are frightened, sad, or deeply uncertain about the future. In those moments, might your five senses offer some pleasure, some support, some relief? Might doing so help take the edge off the challenges of working in education today?

Doing Satisfying Things

The idea of doing satisfying things means choosing actions that provide a sense of accomplishment, fulfillment, or mastery—actions that make you feel good for having gotten them done or that give you a modicum of control in a world seemingly out of control. For example, consider working on a hobby, running a marathon, writing a letter to a friend, or checking three things off your to-do list. Even simple things like washing the dishes, if done mindfully, can give you a sense of satisfaction.

In my case, for as long as I can remember, I've grown some twenty varieties of zinnias from seed each summer. In late winter, I'd order my seeds, and in early April, I'd plant them in little starter pots. For about six weeks, I'd carefully water the seedlings, cull the weakest ones, and then plant the hardiest in my garden. The result was about thirty plants that would provide delight through the summer and early fall. In the midst of a jammed schedule, I somehow found the time to concentrate my energies on zinnias because I knew—perhaps subconsciously—I needed a break.

What gives you a similar pleasure and satisfaction? Might it be gourmet cooking, coaching a kids sports team, or painting watercolors? Perhaps you prefer something a bit zanier, like belly dancing, penning a romance novel, or building wacky birdhouses.

Mark Williams and Danny Penman underscore the importance of doing things that satisfy: "The old saying, 'All work and no play makes Jack a dull boy' contains more than a grain of truth. Many other societies have similar homilies. And in some cultures doctors don't ask, 'When did you start to feel depressed?' but, 'When did you stop dancing?'"[13]

RESTORING PERSPECTIVE

When leaders are up to their eyeballs in work, it's all too easy to get caught up in the daily minutiae and lose any sense of perspective. They can easily forget why they are doing the work—and what life is about. They might lose sight of how others see what is needed and might forget that the seemingly impossible is often possible. When I would hit the wall as dean, I would often make a beeline for a nearby kindergarten and just watch the kids, thereby rekindling my enthusiasm for my work and restoring my sense of perspective.

Many nourishing activities can broaden your own perspective: you could read a history book, visit a different culture, or really try to listen to your colleagues (including those with differing viewpoints), or collect memorable quotes. For example, a pithy quote attributed to Mahatma Gandhi has stuck with me for decades: "I cried because I had no shoes. Then I met a man who had no feet."

Sacred Spaces

Immunologist Esther Sternberg is doing pioneering work on healing spaces (such as hospital rooms overlooking groves of trees rather than concrete walls) and how these special spaces can reduce stress and promote health and well-being. Her research reveals how good design can trigger our "brain's internal pharmacies" and help heal us—and she emphasizes the importance of finding and creating a place of peace. Such sacred spaces can be restorative, broadening our perspectives so we can see things in a new light, both literally and figuratively.[14]

A lovely excerpt from a book citing Virginia Woolf's diaries also captures the importance of sacred spaces in nourishing ourselves and restoring our sense of well-being:

> She seems often to be looking away from Bloomsbury to "the old habitual beauty of England: the silver sheep clustering; and the downs soaring, like birds wings' sweeping up & up . . . It feeds me, rests me, satisfies me as nothing else does . . . This has a holiness. This will go on after I'm dead."

Country walks made her mind "glow like hot iron." She liked to tramp across the downs to the cliffs and glimpse "the gulls on the purple plough" . . . She liked, too, to work at her rug, see to bread-making and preserving, and play bowls on the lawn overlooking the Ouse valley which stretched to Mount Caburn in the distance.[15]

Sacred spaces can be a special place, a beautifully designed building, or just being present in nature and learning what it has to teach, as captured in Mary Oliver's lovely poem "When I Am Among the Trees":

> When I am among the trees,
> especially the willows and the honey locust,
> equally the beech, the oaks and the pines,
> they give off such hints of gladness.
> I would almost say that they save me, and daily.
>
> I am so distant from the hope of myself,
> in which I have goodness, and discernment,
> and never hurry through the world
> but walk slowly, and bow often.
> Around me the trees stir in their leaves
> and call out, "Stay awhile."
> The light flows from their branches.
> And they call again, "It's simple," they say,
> "and you too have come
> into the world to do this, to go easy, to be filled
> with light, and to shine."[16]

For my own sacred spaces, I intentionally seek out beauty—a sunset, a mountain view, a star-filled sky. Savoring exquisite places soothes my soul and restores my sense of perspective. What's more, any chance I get, I head for green spaces bathed in light.

Stillness

In our rush to do things, it's also worth remembering to just be still, to do nothing, to just be. In stressful times, stillness has many benefits, among them restoring your perspective. In the following reflection on Chuang Tzu's "Flight from the Shadow," Mark Bielang, school superintendent of Portage Public Schools in Michigan, highlights the importance of stillness in nourishing yourself:

> There was a man who was so disturbed by the sight of his own shadow and so displeased with his own footsteps that he determined to get rid of both . . .
>
> So he got up and ran. But every time he put his foot down there was another step, while his shadow kept up with him without the slightest difficulty.
>
> . . . [H]e ran faster and faster, without stopping, until he finally dropped dead.
>
> He failed to realize that if he merely stepped into the shade, his shadow would vanish, and if he sat down and stayed still, there would be no more footsteps.
>
> . . . As a superintendent, I consider my to-do list to be my constant companion. It helps keep me focused. It prioritizes my daily activities. It gives me a sense of achievement when I cross off completed tasks. The one thing it doesn't accomplish is to just let me be . . . after all, it's a to-do list, not a to-be list! . . .
>
> "Flight from the Shadow" is the perfect antidote to the frantic pace of everyday life. It reminds me and other district leaders that we must step into the shade, sit down, and stay still.
>
> Being still, even for brief periods of time, gives us the chance to listen to our inner voice, gain broader perspectives, and thus better serve ourselves as well as our students and staff.[17]

N

Bielang's reflection is remarkable not only in suggesting the power of stillness in restoring perspective, but also in demonstrating what it means to set the tone for an organization. Getting the tone right to fit the circumstances is one of the most important and often overlooked roles that leaders have.

BEING GRATEFUL

In your leadership work, how often do you display gratefulness? A call, an email, a face-to-face meeting, a handwritten note expressing genuine appreciation—all can raise spirits, especially if unexpected and not tied to a request. The same is true for random acts of kindness. Gratitude is good for your colleagues and your organization—and although it is often overlooked, expressing appreciation can also have big benefits for you.

A wonderful website, www.gratefulness.org, describes how gratitude can restore us: "Grateful living is a way of life which asks us to notice all that is already present and abundant—from the tiniest things of beauty to the grandest of our blessings—and in so doing, to take nothing for granted. Small, grateful acts every day can uplift us, make a difference for others, and help change the world." If you want a lift right now, take a few minutes to watch "A Good Day," a beautiful video by David Steindl-Rast, a Benedictine monk.[18] "I watch this video so often," says Susan Agrue, an assistant principal of a public school in North Carolina, in an e-mail to me. "It is one of my most favorite things you have ever shared with me. It helps to center me and bring me back to what is true and what is constant."

A practical example of the benefits of gratitude come from a retired head of a special education school, David Hirshberg, who started writing gratitude letters in 1980 and has been doing so ever since. In a recent note to me, he captures the power—for both the recipient and the writer—of putting down on paper words that express appreciation:

These letters were very powerful to the recipients, several of whom told me they saved them forever; some kept them on their refrigerator or fireplace mantel. But what surprised me was its impact on me. I learned that I experienced a surge of affection for the target of the letter as I wrote. The act of forcing myself to get in touch with what I was grateful for, focusing on gratitude, paying attention to what these people have done to help me reach my goals, put me in the best mood imaginable. Although it took me a while to get started (not being a naturally appreciative person), time disappeared. Sometimes I would cry tears of happiness.

Later I hypothesized that maybe when I was disappointed with someone (and I could get stuck there), writing that person a gratitude letter, as counterintuitive as it may seem, might snap me out of it and get the relationship productive again. It worked so well that over time most of my gratitude letters were written in times of deep frustration, always helping me feel more appreciative of the other person, and better about myself—more competent, wise, less stressed out, relieved, a better leader. Writing gratitude letters became a way of taking care of myself.

Writing this kind of letter offers big dividends, especially when the letter is written by hand. The exercise "Penning Handwritten Notes" outlines Hirshberg's recommendation. See if it works for you.

N

PENNING HANDWRITTEN NOTES
(10–60 minutes)

To begin, think of a person who works for you, whether or not you are upset with him or her, and to whom you have not expressed your appreciation or support recently.

Second, describe in specific terms what this person did, what the positive outcomes were for the organization or you, and how that makes you feel. The letter should be just one handwritten paragraph—short and sweet, but clear about what the person did and why it matters to you.

Third, write several letters, three to six, in an hour-long session. (If you don't have an hour to set aside, of course, you can write fewer letters in less time.)

The first letter may be difficult, Hirshberg says, since you will have to make the transition from a critical mind-set to an accepting, supportive, appreciative mind-set. You will need to appreciate what you usually take for granted, and it takes some time to make the shift. But once you do, you might get into a flow where you can rip out several letters of gratitude quickly. After all, your people are trying to please you every day. You just have to adjust your perceptions so that you can see what they have been doing to advance your organization.

TAKING IN THE GOOD

Many of the above experiences can make you feel better, and that's not a trivial result, especially when you are feeling beat and blue. But Rick Hanson convincingly argues that the benefits will be fleeting unless you "consistently and systematically take the extra seconds to *install* these experiences in the brain."[19] If we put in the careful attention, we can learn to rewire the brain, which can have a profound influence on our lives. Indeed, Hanson contends that we can "build a brain strong enough to withstand its ancient negativity bias, allowing contentment and a powerful sense of well-being to become the new normal. In mere minutes each day, we can transform our brains into oases of calm. We can hardwire in happiness."[20]

Now that's a big promise, but Hanson's book carefully reviews the brain science backing his claim, and he teaches us how to "take in the good." His method goes beyond just having positive thoughts and feelings. It entails consciously having lots of good experiences, enriching them through such practices as taking the time to savor your experiences and absorbing them into your very being. He cites positive experiences such as thinking of someone you like or who cares for you, and thinking of things that help you feel strong, peaceful, grateful, loved, and loving.

Hanson sees his approach as a natural extension of mindfulness, which often counsels noticing difficulties and being with them. According to Hanson, taking in the good adds a missing ingredient for healing—namely, not only being with the bad, but also intentionally seeking and being with the good:

> By taking just a few extra seconds to stay with a positive experience—even the comfort in a single breath—you'll help turn a passing mental state into a lasting neural structure. Over time, you can fill up your inner storehouse with the strengths you need, such as feeling at ease rather than irritable, loved rather than mistreated, and resourced rather than running on empty. These strengths will foster well-being and effectiveness, heal psychological issues such as anxiety, and support creativity, self-actualization, and spiritual practice.
>
> ... It's natural to take in the good. We all know its essence: have a positive experience and then really enjoy it. But as with any other skill, you can get better at it through learning and practice.[21]

The following guided practice is an example of what Hanson calls "taking in the good." I have used it with my students for a number of years, before I knew about Hanson's work, and the method has gotten a lot of positive feedback. This exercise is primarily aimed at leaders who regularly arrive at work preoccupied

N

with the relentless pressures of the job. In this state of mind, we can easily forget all the good things in our lives, forget what's going well at work, dwell on what's going wrong, and put our worst foot forward. A bad start can easily spiral into a bad day.

If this pattern rings true for you, the following guided practice, "CVS Morning Pause" (CVS for *counting* blessings, relishing *victories*, and *showing* up), might help you start the day with a broader perspective and a more balanced state of mind. Like CVS pharmacies, the CVS morning pause offers some needed relief.

CVS MORNING PAUSE   *(3–5 minutes)*

Taking a moment to silently express gratitude, and feel it in your bones, can enhance your mood and nurture a positive attitude. So, let's begin by focusing your attention on the blessings in your life.

- *Count your blessings:* When you are ready, ask yourself, "What makes my life worth living? What gives me joy? What am I grateful for? What makes me smile?" You might identify people important to you. Or you might identify your health, new opportunities, or whatever else comes to mind. Now, zoom in on two or three blessings that you want to express gratitude for today. You might silently say something like this: "I'm so lucky to have Susan as a wife. Thanks, Susan," or "I'm so fortunate to have good health." Notice how you feel. For a moment more, count your blessings, and fully take in your warm feelings. Fully savor them.

- *Relish your victories:* Now, shift your attention to any recent victories at work—victories that are perhaps small and private. For example, you might have taken a baby step on a complex project, comforted a grieving colleague, or quietly withstood wrongheaded pressure. Identifying victories is not always easy, because we discount our successes and instead tend to dwell on our setbacks.

So, take a moment to identify just one or two victories. Ponder them. Take deserved pride in what you've accomplished. Take pleasure and satisfaction in things that have worked. Notice how you feel right now. Take a moment to fully savor your positive feelings.

- *Show up as your Light:* Now, ask yourself, "Which parts of me are going to show up at work this morning? My stressed self? My small-minded self? My entangled self? My reactive self?" Instead, imagine showing up as your Light: the part of your mind that's able to step back, notice, and illuminate your small stuff instead of getting swept away by it—the part that's calm, curious, and compassionate. For a moment, ponder your Light. Notice how you feel. Take joy in your wholesome qualities. Now, imagine *being* your Light as you arrive at work later this morning—perhaps with a smile on your face.

Finally, thank your mind for all its hard work: Open your eyes, and return to your day ahead with the intention of making your Light your home base as you put your best foot forward.

A FEW FINAL TIPS

N

Here's a potpourri of additional tips that come from the research literature as well as my own experience:

- *Smile more:* Small changes in your facial muscles can change your mood and lead to emotions that are more positive. Laughter too can be remarkably uplifting, reducing stress and boosting engagement and well-being.
- *Lighten up:* You need not dress up as Santa Claus each December, but you can take steps to be serious without being too serious. Step back and see the funny or ironic side of situations. Introducing humor into the conversation can reduce stress and soothe the soul.

- **Join up:** Don't forget that learning something brand new without the support of other like-minded people is really hard to do. This insight is widespread—from Buddhism, to Alcoholics Anonymous, to the buddy system in the US armed forces, to Weight Watchers. Learning the nourishing steps of MY DANCE is easier if it's not a solo undertaking.

- **Show generosity:** Qualities that represent the opposite of generosity—pettiness of mind and character, meanness of spirit, being stingy with your time and attention—are easily spotted by those you are trying to lead and thereby undermine your legitimate authority. What's more, generosity of spirit rewards not only the recipient, but also those who choose to give. The opportunity to serve others and wholeheartedly share what you have to offer both fosters a better world and makes you feel better, too.

- **Get a dog:** And take Fido to the office, if workplace policies permit. I realize that this tip might not be practicable for many people, but some research shows that dogs at work reduce office stress.[22] Even more, if you crave appreciation at work, truly your best bet is to rely on your pooch!

So, how do you rest and relax? Experience pleasure? Restore your perspective? Experience gratitude? Do you have a sacred space that brings you peace? Do you regularly take in the good? The list of nourishing activities is almost endless—and what works best varies significantly from individual to individual. You need to use whatever wholesome activities—including stillness and silence—work for you, even if the activities initially strike you as self-indulgent, trivial, or eccentric.

In the end, if you fail to nourish yourself, you'll lack the personal reserves—the strength, energy, and positive perspective—to care for others and get the job done. What's more, you deserve nourishment for just being who you are. Just like every other fallible human being who walks the earth, you deserve it.

Indeed, I invite you to give yourself a break, both figuratively and literally, and give yourself permission to engage in wholesome, self-soothing activities. Open your heart to the idea that it's really OK to be struggling with your work and to take steps to care for yourself. Martyrs-'R'-Us is decidedly not the point of this chapter.

N

Cherish Self-Compassion

You will never be all that you can be, until you accept all that you are.

—*Pamela Brooke*

In a Nutshell ...

What This Step Is

- The ability to *give yourself the kindness* you deserve and need, just as you would tender warmth and understanding to a dear friend

What This Step Helps You Do

- Tap into your inner capacity to soothe yourself, thereby reducing the self-rebuke that can make you feel blue and forget what it's like to be fully alive

- Open your heart to wise action: allowing what life brings, accepting personal shortcomings, reaching out for help, and showing others compassion

- Muster the courage, resolve, and resilience to handle life's challenges while moving toward what matters to you with inner balance, good humor, and joy

GIVING MYSELF A GERMER

If truth be told, learning the skill of self-compassion has been a godsend for me. It has taken the edge off what has been the toughest time in my personal life. I start by recounting my story at home because I believe it conveys important lessons for those of us facing different, but similarly daunting challenges at work. I'm thinking of moments like when an unexpected crisis threatens your organization's future, your most important initiative becomes a whopping failure, your school has just lost some major funding, or a new boss undercuts everything you've worked for and stand for. Perhaps self-compassion, the ability to be kind to yourself, will also be a godsend for you.

On November 20, 2012, a day I'll never forget, my wife Susan was diagnosed with Alzheimer's disease. After a few minutes of testing, a prominent Boston neurologist announced his conclusion and immediately asked for questions, showing nary a hint of warmth or compassion. We were distraught, hardly able to utter a coherent word. Even though Susan's memory lapses had brought us to the hospital, we were unprepared for the abruptness and finality of the diagnosis. We returned home in a daze, canceled a Thanksgiving Day outing two days later, and spent the long weekend at home licking our wounds, trying to care for each other, and worrying about what was to come.

I was scheduled, about two weeks later, to colead a four-day Harvard workshop for seventy-plus principals, deans, school superintendents, and other education leaders. My first impulse was to bow out, but it was too late to find a replacement. Instead, I decided to steer clear of my usual personal anecdotes in any of my presentations, fearing I'd be unable to hold myself together. So, I buried my raw feelings during public sessions, maintained a facade of good cheer, and retreated to my office during breaks to let my emotions run free.

During the workshop, I was especially moved by one guest speaker, the psychologist and self-compassion expert Christopher Germer. After he finished his presentation on self-compassion, I accompanied him outside to say thanks and good-bye. I told Chris how deeply touched I was by his talk—and then burst into uncontrollable tears. As I stood there shaking, mumbling a few words about my wife's disease, Chris enveloped me in his arms. He simply held me steady with a warm embrace while emitting a few soothing sounds. No advice, no pep talk, no questions. After a few moments, my tears subsided and we quietly parted. I pulled myself together, wiped my cheeks, and returned to the workshop, surprisingly renewed and ready to get back to work.

Later, I chuckled over the odd scene we must have presented to faculty colleagues passing by the library that cold winter afternoon: a tall young man with a silver mane hugging a sobbing former dean. Little did onlookers know they were witnessing a moment of pure compassion. Even more, little did I know the healing power of compassion until I felt Chris's comforting response deep in my bones—and contrasted his caring manner with that of the robotic neurologist who had given my wife and me her diagnosis two weeks earlier.

As the shock has receded, Susan and I are striving to accept reality with grace. We count our blessings and even savor silver linings. We've begun to come to terms with the excruciating loss of her beautiful mind, her independence, and her dreams for retirement. I've witnessed up close Susan's heartbreaking pain and bravery. And I've learned about the essence of compassion— just being there, without an agenda, for someone in need—just as Chris was there for me.

As Susan's disease advances, I've thought a lot about what it will take for me to be her steady anchor. I've come to internalize what the books say: being kind to oneself is a prerequisite for showing compassion for others. Why is this true? Well, think

C

about it this way: if you feel like you're about to drown, your survival instincts make it impossible to extend a helping hand to another drowning person. But self-compassion provides the life raft, a safe place from where you can address your basic needs *and* reach out to others with kindness.

Susan's disease has been tough on me, no doubt about it, especially in my role as primary caregiver. Even with the help of several wonderful friends and caregivers, the devotion of her family in North Carolina, and the support of a fine medical team, I often feel as if I'm drowning in a sea of new responsibilities and emotional demands. And when I'm really going under, my heart is often closed to being the kind husband I want to be.

The easier part of caregiving has been handling the growing demands on my time: managing the family chores, countless visits to doctors and hospitals, regular searches for a misplaced cell phone, scheduling outings with friends—while also finding the time and energy to teach part time, not to mention finish this book. Often I feel like a novice funambulist, regularly falling off the new tightrope I now so unexpectedly walk.

The tougher part of caregiving, however, is handling those experiences that drain my emotional reserves and my energy. For one, it's really hard to watch my spouse of forty-six years lose her mind; at times, the sadness can be overwhelming. For another, I often feel like a lifeguard on round-the-clock duty. Even when I've carved out time to write, a sliver of my brain is constantly scanning the soundscape for noises that signal that Susan may be in peril. Other times, I feel like the guardian of a precious crystal vase—beautiful to behold, but increasingly fragile: with an unexpected ping, Susan can shatter into shards.

Most challenging has been showing love when Susan is the least lovable, when she needs compassion the most as her disease-driven brain lashes out at the world—and at me, the person she depends on the most to hold a safe place for her agitation, her disorientation, her anger, her terrible sense of loss. All this is incredibly hard on Susan and upsetting and exhausting for me. And it's sobering to be told that the worst is yet to come.

Here's where the skill of self-compassion comes into play. When I feel like I'm about to drown, I turn to four phrases I've memorized—a long mantra of sorts—to help guide me through the storm. This mantra is adapted from the groundbreaking work of Kristin Neff, and I'll use it here to summarize what self-compassion means to me:

> This is a tough moment
> Tough moments are inescapable
> Tough moments call out for tender care
> I'll give myself the kindness I deserve—and need.[1]

I keep a copy of this mantra on my smartphone for ready use in case my memory fails me. I use it mainly when dealing with my particular situation at home, but I believe it is equally applicable in dealing with the emotional demands of leading at work. Perhaps you too might develop a similar mantra; I encourage you to find your own words, those that work best for you, given your particular situation and sensibilities.

Each of these four phrases speaks to a different aspect of self-compassion. The first phrase—"This is a tough moment"—points to the importance of pausing in the midst of experiencing a really tough time. The basic idea is to stop what we're doing and acknowledge the reality of our situation—to neither suppress the pain nor wallow in it, but to gently accept it and make room for it.

The second phrase—"Tough moments are inescapable"—helps us keep perspective by reminding us that *everyone* faces tough moments at times. Even more, the world is filled with people who are a lot worse off than we are. This phrase is an antidote to the why-me syndrome, a counterweight to the oft-heard cry "I just want my life back," and is the very opposite of self-pity. It reminds us that we are all flawed human beings grappling with

C

what life throws at us and trying to do our best, knowing that some days will be better than others.

The third phrase—"Tough moments call out for tender care"—is a reminder that wounds require balm to heal. It's not self-indulgent to care for ourselves, in just the way we would care for a dear friend in need. Indeed, leaders often need to be reminded that self-care is a sign of strength, not weakness, even if our culture often teaches us to suppress our feelings and just keep a stiff upper lip.

The fourth phrase—"I'll give myself the kindness I deserve and need"—is a call to action, a commitment to do what we can to heal our wounds. It reminds us that all human beings deserve kindness as their birthright and, most important, that we all need kindness to be at our best in a difficult world. And it's a reminder to do those specific things that soothe us, that nourish our soul.

In these moments, I offer myself kindness in three ways: with soothing words and thoughts, with a compelling image, and with comforting actions. The most soothing words I use are "No wonder," a short phrase recommended by Ann Weiser Cornell.[2] In acknowledging a tough time, I might say to myself, "There's something in me that's completely overwhelmed right now. No wonder, given everything that's on my plate." Here's another example of a comforting thought: "It's OK not to be OK."

The most compelling image for me is the memory of being warmly embraced by Chris Germer outside the library door. I can still vividly picture the scene and intentionally recall it in the midst of a tough time. It may sound corny, but I say to myself, "It's time to give myself a Germer." The most soothing actions for me are to put a gentle hand on my heart, to start the day with a soothing hot shower, and to seek out places of beauty in nature—to name just three. Not to mention the comfort and perspective I find in writing.

Self-compassion has helped me survive and even flourish in the midst of huge challenges. It has helped me open my heart to my wife and avoid defining my life by circumstances beyond my control. For sure, I'm not always able to dance in the rain. But I can count more good days than I ever would have thought possible before I began to learn self-compassion. Indeed, it just might be a secret sauce for me—and for many education professionals as well.

LOOKING BACK—AND FORWARD

In earlier chapters, I spotlighted a life-changing new way to relate to your experiences—namely, being with them moment by moment with openness, curiosity, and acceptance, in the service of living a vital life aimed at doing what matters most to you as a leader, an educator, and a human being. In chapter 9, the main focus shifted from your *experiences* to you the *experiencer*. I introduced some simple ways you can start nourishing yourself. In this chapter, I zero in on a particularly important form of nourishment: self-compassion. In fact, during the last few years, research on self-compassion has skyrocketed; today, scores of studies support the commonsense notion that being kind to yourself is both important and effective for living a full and healthy life.[3]

Self-compassion is important as a stand-alone activity, and increasingly it's being recognized as going hand in glove with mindfulness. "The truth is that mindfulness cannot be reduced to awareness or attention alone," say Zindel Segal and colleagues. Its effectiveness "depends on whether friendliness and compassion can be brought to those elements of present-moment experience to which we attend."[4] In simpler terms, in doing the work of MY DANCE, we need to bring both greater attention to the experience and greater warmth to the experiencer.

To give you a better sense of self-compassion, this first brief exercise, "From Fist to Palm," contrasts the benefits of self-compassion with the debilitating effects of its opposite, self-rebuke. The exercise illustrates how we often mishandle our difficult thoughts and feelings by beating ourselves up for falling short. The remaining exercises help you examine the nature and benefits of self-compassion, explore why so many of us resist it, and learn how to develop this skill.

FROM FIST TO PALM   (3–5 minutes)

Imagine that your hands contain all your difficult thoughts and feelings—all the emotional stuff that keeps you awake at night. Now, if you can, turn your attention to the kinds of situations or circumstances when you engage in excessive self-criticism, when you beat yourself up for falling short. Take a moment to recall some of your difficult thoughts and feelings, and imagine holding them in your hands.

Now, imagine metaphorically beating yourself up by turning your hands into fists and thumping yourself about your head. While doing so, ponder these questions: When I get entangled in all my stuff, do I blame myself for things gone awry—and beat myself up for falling short? Would I treat a dear friend this way, if he or she were in need? Do I really believe—deep down—that this self-flagellation will make things better? When I am preoccupied with my shortcomings, am I distracted from what matters most to me in life? Do I sidetrack the energy and focus to show compassion for others?

When you are ready, open your hands and gently place them in your lap. Now, visualize using your hands in a different way. Instead of thumping yourself, put a gentle hand on your heart or on the part of you that hurts, just as you might gently rub an ache on a child's back. In doing so, might you experience the warmth of your touch? Might you welcome this act of kindness and self-compassion?

Again, notice the difference between fist and palm. Are you less distracted when your hands relax and caress? Perhaps less tired? Notice how much easier it is to do the things that matter to you, like caring for others. Also, you'll probably find that your self-criticism hasn't totally disappeared. It is still with you, but you are responding to it differently. As a result, it has much less influence over you. You can do the things you value without being derailed by all your heavy stuff.

When you are ready, slowly bring your attention back to the room, and return to your day ahead with the intention of showing more compassion for yourself when the going gets tough.

As you may have noticed, this is the third exercise using your hands to illustrate the negative effects of the three Rs. While here I focus on self-rebuke, earlier I used the metaphor of the hands to illustrate the effects of the other two Rs—resistance to upsetting feelings and excessive rumination. If you like, take a moment to review these three hands exercises, all of which emphasize the visual and the kinesthetic. Taken together, they illustrate the promise of MY DANCE for handling difficulties.

- Instead of covering your eyes with your hands and becoming obsessed with your heavy stuff, create some distance by lowering your hands, and thereby gain some perspective on your troubling experiences.
- Instead of pushing your hands up, up, and away, in an effort to resist and get rid of all your difficulties, calmly place your hands in your lap and allow the heavy stuff of life just to be there, exactly as it is.
- Instead of thumping yourself in self-reproach for your perceived faults and failures, gently place your hands on your heart or the place that hurts.

C

Instead of being a slave to your heavy stuff and mishandling it, you can free your hands and take action guided by your values.

WHAT IT'S ALL ABOUT

To understand self-compassion and its benefits, it's helpful to briefly survey the work of several well-known pioneers who come to self-compassion from different scientific orientations. My understanding has been most influenced by psychologists Christopher Germer, Paul Gilbert, and Kristin Neff.

Paul Gilbert, the creator of compassion-focused therapy (CFT), has captured in a few words the essence of self-compassion and why it matters: "Self-compassion is a way of being with ourselves in all our emotions, uncomfortable as they may be, without self-condemning and instead with support and encouragement. Research shows the more compassionate we are toward ourselves, the happier we are and the more resilient we become when faced with difficult events in our lives. In addition, we are able to reach out to others for help, and feel more compassionate toward other people, too."[5]

Gilbert's work has been pivotal in illuminating how human brains, evolved over millions of years, can get in our own way—for example, by overreacting to threats with excessive worry. He shows that at the same time, our brains have within them the innate capacity to soothe us in times of distress. He has developed numerous techniques for accessing our human capacity to comfort and heal ourselves.[6]

Kristin Neff is also an influential academician, in part because she offers a compelling and accessible explanation of what self-compassion is and why it is so important. Self-compassion, she says, involves three key elements: self-kindness, a sense of our common humanity, and mindfulness. By self-kindness, she means "being warm and understanding toward ourselves when we suffer, fail, or feel inadequate, rather than ignoring our pain or flagellating ourselves with self-criticism."[7] Neff emphasizes that we are all imperfect and cannot always get what we want: "When this reality is accepted with kindness, greater emotional equanimity is experienced."

Neff also contends that when we do not get what we want—when we fall short—our frustration is "often accompanied by an irrational but pervasive sense of isolation—as if 'I' were the only person suffering or making mistakes." She says that, as humans, we all suffer, and "the very definition of being 'human' means that one is mortal, vulnerable, and imperfect . . . [S]elf-compassion involves recognizing that suffering and personal inadequacy is part of the shared human experience—something that we all go through rather than something that happens to 'me' alone."

Neff advocates a balanced and mindful approach to negative thoughts and emotions "so that feelings are neither suppressed nor exaggerated." We must be willing to observe them "with openness and clarity, so that they are held in mindful aware-ness." If they are suppressed, we can't feel compassion for them. If they are exaggerated, we can get "caught up and swept away by negative reactivity."

Neff has recently teamed up with Germer to create the Cen-ter for Mindful Self-Compassion, an effort specifically designed to teach self-compassion skills. These skills, it turns out, have much to offer education leaders. "Mindful self-compassion is the foundation of emotional healing," says Germer. "[It] can be learned by anyone. It's the practice of repeatedly evoking good will toward ourselves especially when we're suffering—cultivat-ing the same desire that all living beings have to live happily and free from suffering. And as the Dalai Lama says, self-compassion is the first step toward compassion for others."[8]

Buddhist teacher Mathieu Ricard and his colleagues make a crucial distinction between the effects of empathy and compas-sion in our dealings with others. (In colloquial terms, empathy is putting yourself in the shoes of another, while compassion

C

has the added dimension of taking action to alleviate the suffering.) The authors suggest that negative emotions like emotional exhaustion, or burnout, are "in fact a kind of 'empathy fatigue.'"[9] On the other hand, compassion is associated with positive emotions. Indeed, "compassion, far from leading to distress and discouragement reinforces an inner balance, strength of mind, and a courageous determination to help those who suffer." It's the difference between an empathic school principal who is overwhelmed by distress and societal injustice and gives up in despair and a compassionate principal working to comfort and help disadvantaged children succeed in school. The empathic principal is a good candidate for burnout, "which, in one US study, beset[s] about 60 percent of the 600 caregivers surveyed."

A HARD SELL—AND BEYOND

For all the talk these days about the importance of self-compassion, it nevertheless remains a hard sell, perhaps especially for those in leadership positions in education and other helping professions. Why so? In this section, I discuss several personal barriers to self-compassion. I then invite you to consider an alternative perspective that could make self-compassion a more integral part of your life. Of course, you need to decide for yourself if this perspective is helpful to you, your colleagues, and your organization. Only if you buy into the importance of self-compassion will you put in the effort to develop the skill.

To start, self-compassion is a hard sell because it contradicts what many of us have been taught since childhood about how to make it in our highly competitive world. To get to the top, the prevailing wisdom says, we need to be ambitious, self-centered, and focused on outperforming others; compassion takes a back seat or is often ignored altogether. You may adopt a veneer of compassion to look human in public, but society truly values individual productivity and perfectionism, not warmth and compassion—or so we have been led to believe.

Self-compassion is also a hard sell because of our personal fears, one of which is the fear of losing our edge. If we don't hold ourselves strictly accountable, we will become lazy, lose our motivation, and diminish our productivity. A related fear is that of imperfection. If we are not relentlessly self-critical, so the thinking goes, we will screw up and fall short of meeting the needs of our classrooms, schools, or other organizations. And then there is the powerful fear of feeling weak—even worse, of appearing weak. After all, we have been brought up to believe that leaders are supposed to be hard-headed, decisive, and strong. They should "power through" their emotions and not engage in "soft," self-indulgent activities that steal time from the real work of getting results and getting ahead.

In addition to these various fears, many of us are loath to embrace self-compassion because we don't think we deserve it, given our self-perception of our faults and failures and the often-accompanying shame. Being kind to ourselves is particularly difficult when we're in a lot of pain, says Buddhist teacher and writer Pema Chödrön, "where we feel ashamed, as if we don't belong, as if we've just blown it, when things are falling apart for us."[10]

If self-compassion is a hard sell in general, it may be especially hard for people working in education, for three reasons. First, the widespread perception of unworthiness may well be exacerbated for school leaders because it's easy some days to feel like a fraud. Running a school or school system, for example, requires you to make big promises about what you can accomplish while you know deep down you can't "fix" the kids by just fixing the schools. The paradox can sometimes make you feel like a fake—and fakers don't deserve compassion from themselves or from anyone else.

Second, other leaders in education are allergic to self-compassion because they believe self-compassion is the wrong thing to do—an improper and unprofessional expenditure of their time. "Even a sin," says a former high school teacher. After all, education professionals are caregivers, and there's never enough time to care for the students, who are so needy and deserving of attention. On top of that, if you are a principal or school superintendent, you need to care for the caregivers, the teachers who are often exhausted from their life-altering work with children. With all these demands for caregiving, how can we possibly take our precious—and limited—time and shower it on ourselves? I've witnessed this phenomenon often enough to know that it can be a powerful obstacle to self-compassion for conscientious educators.

And finally, some education leaders steer clear of self-compassion because they've never learned how to do it. Nor have they been encouraged—or given permission—to do so in their professional training. They've been so single-mindedly focused on serving their students that they've never learned the skills. An education professional once told me that he was advised by his doctor to take better care of himself, given everything on his plate. He had never cared for himself, he told me, because there was never time to do so—and he simply didn't know how to do it.

Given this wariness about compassion, and especially self-compassion, what's the case for those of us learning to be more self-compassionate, for bucking the view that self-compassion is self-indulgent or just a self-pity party, for getting out of our own way and showing kindness toward ourselves?

First off, the chief fears about the disadvantages of self-compassion are ungrounded. In fact, research shows that self-compassion and judicious self-criticism are helpful, but as Neff and Germer point out, "harsh and belittling self-criticism is not: it tends to make people depressed and lose self-confidence . . . [S]elf-compassionate people aim just as high as those who lack self-compassion, but don't become as distressed and frustrated when they can't meet their goals. They are also more likely to pick themselves up and try again after failing."[11] And as to the fear of feeling weak, as I have suggested throughout this book, we need to redefine what we mean by leadership strength. It is not a matter of overpowering our emotions; instead, we need to recognize them, befriend them, and cut ourselves some slack.

Moreover, we are all deserving of compassion because, as human beings, we all occasionally make mistakes, fall short of our ideals, and do things that we are ashamed of. Though we may not like to admit it, all of us lead far-from-perfect lives.

Jeff Young, the superintendent of the Cambridge Public Schools, shared with me a question he was once asked by his perplexed kids: "They put you in charge of a $160 million budget—do they know what a dork you are?" With a smile, Young shares this question with his colleagues to remind them—and to remind himself—that he's just a regular human being. And when he goes home at night, to avoid self-rebuke and to live with himself, he says to himself, "I'm just a guy. I did the best I could today." He also reminds himself that there's a huge difference between intent and effect, and he can't hold himself accountable for outcomes he can't control.

Young's nuanced outlook reminds me of *wabi-sabi*, a conspicuous feature of traditional Japanese art that also serves as a worldview, one centered on finding beauty, not fault, in imperfection. "Through wabi-sabi," says writer Robyn Griggs Lawrence, "we learn to embrace liver spots, rust, and frayed edges, and the march of time they represent."[12] At its core, self-compassion grows out of an acceptance of ourselves just the way we are, warts and all.[13] And surprisingly, this embrace of our imperfections is a precursor to personal change. "The curious paradox," Carl Rogers famously said, "is that when I accept myself just as I am, then I can change."

Self-compassion is not only a good thing to do, but it is also the right thing to do, the professional thing to do. We all know the emergency instructions on airplanes—put on your oxygen mask first before you try to help others. Why? Because if you don't take care of yourself, you'll be ineffective with others. Self-compassion is an act of compassion for others.

It takes courage to buck widespread views that devalue self-compassion, because to do so is to invite ridicule. What's more, the common view is partly right—leading successfully does take ambition, drive, laser-like focus, and a deep concern with productivity. In my view, instead of rejecting this societal view, it makes practical sense to balance it with a focus on compassion. Besides its moral underpinnings, compassion is an integral part of being a leader in caregiving organizations like schools. It also enhances your chances of living a life marked by meaning, purpose, and vitality, not just by material success that regularly leaves us wanting more from life.

In the end, less is more; the less time you spend rebuking yourself, the more you will accomplish—and flourish. Self-compassion is essential in nurturing yourself and thereby maintaining your high spirits, emotional balance, and resilience. It is also essential in your dealings with others—indeed, if you are preoccupied with self-criticism, then self-rebuke will only undermine your relations with others. This MY DANCE step is central to your own flourishing and to the flourishing of your organization.

DEVELOPING SELF-COMPASSION

As with the other skills of MY DANCE, it is one thing to read about self-compassion and quite another to develop the skill. Fortunately, the interest in self-compassion among researchers and practitioners in the West has led to many excellent research studies, publications, exercises, and programs specifically focused on the skill.[14]

In this section, I'll introduce two of my favorite guided practices to give you a flavor of the inventive exercises out there. I'll also present a meditation designed to extend warm wishes to yourself and others. And then I'll conclude with a personal story that addresses self-compassion and several other steps of MY DANCE. (The "Further Reading and Other Resources" section at the end of the book suggests resources on fully developing your skills in self-compassion.)

To start, Germer reminds us that it is a human condition to be imperfect—and to feel bad about it. All of us at times feel insecure, ashamed, or not good enough. Feelings of failure or inadequacy are part of the experience of being a human being—and of working in education. The "Kind Letter to Myself" exercise, adapted from Germer's work, can help you gain perspective on your harsh self-judgments.[15]

KIND LETTER TO MYSELF *(20–30 minutes)*

Begin by identifying a work issue that makes you feel inadequate or otherwise bad about yourself. Perhaps you feel shy in public forums, have poor relationships with colleagues, or think you really screwed up a project. Take a moment to experience how this issue makes you feel on the inside—for example, sad, angry, embarrassed. Now, write down what you are feeling, being as honest as you can. These words are for your eyes only, so try not to edit what comes up.

Now, shift gears and imagine a friend (or a favorite relative) who is loving and compassionate. Imagine that this friend, who cares deeply about you, can see all your strengths and weaknesses, including the aspects that you have just been writing about. Reflect on this friend's feelings toward you and how you are accepted exactly as you are, with all your human imperfections. This friend recognizes the limits of human nature and is kind and forgiving toward you. He or

C

she understands your life history and recognizes that your perceived inadequacy is connected to so many things you didn't choose: your genes, your family history, life circumstances—things outside your control.

Using the perspective of this imaginary friend, write a letter to yourself, focusing on your perceived inadequacy. What would this friend say to you about your "flaws" from the perspective of unlimited compassion? How would this friend convey the deep compassion felt for you, especially for the pain you feel when you judge yourself so harshly? What would this friend write to remind you that you are only human, that all people have both strengths and weaknesses? And if you think this friend would suggest possible changes you should make, how would these suggestions embody feelings of understanding and compassion? Try to infuse your letter with the strong sense of acceptance, kindness, and desire for your health and happiness that your friend feels for you.

After writing the letter, put it aside for a little while—or, alternatively, you might mail the letter to yourself. Then come back and read it again, letting the words really sink in. Feel the compassion as it pours into you, soothing and comforting you like a cool breeze on a hot day. Love, connection, and acceptance are your birthright. To claim them, you need only look within yourself.

Now, let's go to "Soften, Soothe, Allow," another guided practice adapted from Germer's writings.[16] You can practice this meditation over and over again whenever you feel stress on the job. Our muscles naturally contract when we are under stress; for example, we might experience shortness of breath or muscle tension. By intentionally practicing the following exercise, we can reverse the body's instinctive tendency to resist and react to emotional discomfort. We can also anchor our emotions in the body and transform them there.

SOFTEN, SOOTHE, ALLOW (5–10 minutes)

To begin, "soften" into that location in your body where you can feel the tension. Let the muscles be soft without a requirement that they become soft, like simply applying heat to sore muscles. You can say, "Soften . . . soften . . . soften," quietly to yourself, to enhance the process. Remember that you are not trying to make the uncomfortable sensations go away—you're just being with them with loving awareness. You can also soften at the edges of this area of your body—no need to go right into it.

Now, soothe yourself for struggling in this way. Put your hand over your heart, and feel your body breathe. Perhaps some kind words arise in your mind, such as, "Gee, this is such a painful experience. May I grow in ease and well-being." If you wish, you can also direct kindness to the part of your body that is under stress by placing your hand on that place. It may help to think of your body as if it were the body of a beloved child. You can say kind words to yourself, or just repeat, "Soothe . . . soothe . . . soothe."

Finally, allow the discomfort to be there. Abandon your wish for the feeling to disappear. Let the discomfort come and go as it pleases, like a guest in your own home. You can repeat, "Allow . . . allow . . . allow."

"Soften, soothe, and allow." "Soften, soothe, and allow." You can use these three words like a mantra, reminding yourself to incline with tenderness toward your discomfort.

C

The following exercise, "Warm Wishes," is another meditation to help you experience the goodwill and warmth that lie at the heart of self-compassion. This guided meditation goes back more than twenty-five hundred years and offers warm feelings to you and to others you identify. It is a version of what is traditionally called a loving-kindness meditation, which can be easily found on the Internet and in countless books and recordings. Pema Chödrön says that loving-kindness "means sticking with ourselves when we don't have anything, when we feel like a loser. And it becomes the basis for extending the same unconditional friendliness with others."[17]

I call this meditation "Warm Wishes" for two reasons: In my experience, the term *loving-kindness* can be off-putting to some hard-nosed professionals not steeped in a Buddhist tradition. Also, the idea of extending warm wishes better captures for me what this meditation is about—namely, offering to yourself and to others the gift of acceptance, kindness, and good wishes, with the respect and warmth that we all deserve.

This exercise is my preferred version at the moment. It emphasizes loved ones in my immediate and extended family who are experiencing tough times. I have modified the traditional phrases ("May I be free from danger," "May I have mental happiness," "May I have physical happiness," and "May I have ease of well-being") to include phrases that work better for me. And I've moved the focus on myself to the end of the exercise, rather than the beginning, because doing so makes me more comfortable, particularly in the context of familial sickness. Jack Kornfield, founding teacher of the Insight Meditation Society and Spirit Rock center, helps explain this preference: "In our culture, people find it difficult to direct loving-kindness to themselves . . . So rather than start loving-kindness practice with ourselves, which is traditional, I find it more helpful to start with those we most naturally love and care about."[18]

This meditation aims to extend warm wishes to various individuals and groups by repeating specific phrases. Feel free to vary the phrases you use, the recipients of your warm wishes, and the sequence of wishes you offer. For my own personal meditation, I have made changes to the traditional approach. You too can experiment with adjustments to see what has the most resonance for you.

WARM WISHES   *(2–20 minutes)*

As usual, take a moment to get comfortable in a quiet place where you won't be disturbed. Sit in an erect position that makes you feel both relaxed and alert. Close your eyes, if you like. Place your feet flat on the floor, with your hands in your lap. Let yourself become fully grounded in the earth. Be present in this moment. Right here. Right now.

When you are ready, bring your attention to a close friend or a member of your immediate family—someone whom you would like to focus on for a moment. With this person, or these people, in mind, you might offer these wishes:

- May you be safe and free from harm.
- May you be as happy and healthy as you can be.
- May you be kind to yourself.
- May you dance in the rain of life.

Stay with these words, and the people you have in mind, for as long as you wish. Savor these expressions of respect and affection. Notice what arises in your heart, your body, your mind.

When you are ready, turn your attention, if you wish, to members of your extended family. Keep one family member or more in mind, and repeat these phrases:

- May you be safe and free from harm.
- May you be as happy and healthy as you can be.
- May you be kind to yourself.
- May you dance in the rain of life.

Again, stay with these words, and whomever you have in mind, for as long as you wish. Savor these expressions of respect and affection. And again, notice what arises in your heart, your body, your mind.

When you are ready, and if you have the time and inclination, broaden your attention to your friends and colleagues. Keep these people in mind, and repeat these phrases:

C

- May you be safe and free from harm.
- May you be as happy and healthy as you can be.
- May you be kind to yourself.
- May you dance in the rain of life.

Stay with these words, and the persons in mind, for as long as you wish. Savor these expressions of respect and affection. Notice what arises in your heart, your body, your mind.

Finally, bring your attention back to yourself, and repeat these (slightly modified) phrases:

- May I be safe and free from harm.
- May I be as happy and healthy as I can be.
- May I be kind to myself.
- May I dance in the rain of life.

Stay with these words, and with yourself, for as long as you wish. Savor these expressions of respect and affection. Notice what arises in your heart, your body, your mind.

When you are ready, open your eyes, take a stretch, and return to your day ahead with the intention of extending warm wishes to all those you encounter during the day.

The meditation you just read can be expanded or contracted depending on the time available and the circumstances. What's more, it can be melded into ordinary activities such as taking a shower, going for a walk, or standing in an elevator. Traditionally, you begin the meditation with yourself and follow with someone who has helped you, then a close friend, then a stranger, and then someone you find difficult. The meditation ends with good wishes toward all sentient beings. Again, the byword is the same: craft your very own words, and direct them to whom you want to offer a gift of, yes, unashamed kindness and love.

BAG OF STONES

Let me conclude this chapter with the story of another practice I've used for years to help remind me to show compassion for myself in dealing with the realities of living on earth. This story also helps me remember two other steps of MY DANCE: to *allow unease* and just take it along with me, and to *mind my values*. In pondering this practice, leaders should remember the distinction I explored earlier between the *stress* of poison ivy and the *mind-made misery* caused by scratching the itch. The former is an inevitable part of life; the latter is avoidable.

About five years ago, I bought a small bag—a dark green six-by-eight-inch sports sack—that I initially called my *bag of pain*. Inside, I placed index cards with the following written on separate cards: STRESS, FEARS, ANXIETIES, FEELINGS OF SADNESS AND LOSS, FAILURES, and DISAPPOINTMENTS. Practically everywhere I go, I carry my bag of pain with me in my trusty knapsack. My pain is always with me. It's not something I'm trying to get rid of, but part of what I bring to leadership. It's not something I'm beating myself up for feeling, but it is part of my life. Most of the time, I forget that my bag of pain is in my knapsack. By not resisting it, by not "scratching the itch," I reduce its influence without denying its existence.

Recently, it dawned on me that not only did I carry my pain with me, but I also carried my heartfelt values, which are so easy to forget in stressful situations. So, I decided to add index cards with some of my core values written on them: SERVICE, LIFELONG LEARNING, KINDNESS, SHOWING UP, and THINKING OTHERWISE. I also decided to rename my bag of pain. It is now called my *bag of stones*. For sure, I am weighed down by the heavy stones of life, the inevitable difficulties and disappointments we all encounter. But I also carry with me beautiful stones, my enduring values that glitter like diamonds and lighten my life. I know that's corny

C

(by now you should know that I'm corny!), but the metaphor truly helps me remember what I want to remember.

More recently, I've updated and uploaded the contents of my bag of stones onto my smartphone—more on that later. But in addition to the electronic tool, my little green sports bag of stones continues to be my constant companion. Luddite that I may be, the physical bag is a powerful, tangible reminder that in spite of—or because of—my fallibilities, I can give and receive compassion.

Might you consider creating your very own bag of stones— and bring it along with you, just as you carry your wallet? You could put your own special words on separate index cards—or perhaps a sentence or two that spell out your values and your stressful memories, emotions, and thoughts. Your bag of stones can remind you that you are a fallible human being, like every- one else, and that you are worthy of compassion as you try to reach for the stars with what you've got. And remember, your identity—who you are, what you care about, what you do, what you stand for—need not be defined by just the heavy stones in this little bag in your knapsack.

CHAPTER ELEVEN

Express Feelings Wisely

One can be the master of what one does,
but never of what one feels.

—Gustave Flaubert

In a Nutshell ...

What This Step Is

- The ability to skillfully reveal your human side at work—upsets, vulnerabilities, and joys, as well as empathy and compassion—without undermining your authority

What This Step Helps You Do

- Earn trust, credibility, and respect as a result of your authenticity, which is key in building strong relationships and strong organizations
- Clarify for others what you stand for and why, by acting as a whole human being who experiences—and skillfully expresses—the ups and downs of everyday life
- Ensure that your colleagues feel seen, heard, and respected—and feel that "we are all in this together," which can bring out their best

E

FAITH AND BEGORRA!

I was in a jam. I unexpectedly needed the swift approval of Harvard's president for a new project at the school of education. As dean, I called the president's can-do secretary to see if a short meeting was possible right away. Not surprisingly, the president's schedule was packed, so the assistant suggested a workaround: ride with him to his appointment the next day at the State Street Bank in Boston. She told me to rendezvous with the president's driver, Timmy O'Sullivan, outside the president's office right before it was time to leave.

I got to Massachusetts Hall early and noticed a gentleman standing in the corner of the vestibule. Guessing it was Timmy, I introduced myself, and we immediately hit it off, swapping stories about our common Irish heritage, comparing notes on the counties in Ireland from where our ancestors came, chatting about working at Harvard, and telling a joke or two. When the president arrived, we walked swiftly to his car. I could only imagine the president's thoughts about this invasion of his private space, a rare moment for a busy boss to be alone and think, even to catch a wink.

With the president and me in the back seat and Timmy at the wheel, I immediately launched into my pitch, knowing it would be a quick trip to Boston. It took a while to explain the situation and how my project was in Harvard's best interest. As usual, the president was gracious and asked a series of pointed questions. After a fruitful back and forth, he approved my request—and then almost immediately, like magic, Timmy pulled up in front of the bank. What great timing, I thought.

When we returned to Cambridge, Timmy volunteered to drop me off at the Graduate School of Education. We both got out of the car, and I thanked Timmy for his courtesy and good cheer and expressed my pleasure in meeting him.

He returned the acknowledgment and then, with a twinkle in his eye and a thick Irish brogue, said, "Ah, Dean Murphy, I could tell it was taking a while for you to persuade the president, and we were early for the meeting, so I drove around the block three times until you were done."

"Faith and begorra!" I exclaimed. "Timmy, you are the best."

I tell this story because this chapter is about showing your human side as an education leader, expressing your feelings wisely, and wearing your heart on your sleeve when appropriate. Without being disloyal to his boss, Timmy helped me with a few extra minutes, perhaps because we share a common heritage. But mainly, I believe, he did it because I treated him with respect, curiosity, and interest. He could feel my warm feelings toward him. He could tell I was a regular guy trying to do my job the best I could, just like him.

TAKING STOCK

So far, we've focused on addressing three big challenges that can transform your leadership and life:

- doing what matters most to you: the activities that give you a sense of meaning and purpose
- getting out of your own way by curbing the natural human tendency to respond to discomfort with the three Rs: resistance to the way things are, excessive rumination about our difficulties, and self-rebuke when some things inevitably go awry
- giving yourself permission to take care of yourself because you deserve it and because self-care opens the door to being of service to others

If you get better at addressing these three challenges taken together, you'll get a lot better at dancing in the rain of leadership—and life. Not a bad outcome in a job—and a world—filled with stress.

E

In this chapter, we explore the final step of MY DANCE by switching our focus from the internal world to how to handle our feelings in the external world. In my view, the delicate art of leading is built on a foundation of wisely revealing our human side—including our personal vulnerabilities and our empathy and compassion for others—in ways that enhance our credibility and authority. In what follows, I describe how leaders can, when appropriate, drop their masks at the office, name their feelings instead of showing or hiding them, and express their feelings indirectly. It's possible for leaders both to display warmth and to handle difficult circumstances where they might be particularly prone to blurt out something that they later wish they hadn't.

DROPPING YOUR MASK

As discussed in earlier chapters, it's futile—and usually counter-productive—to try to control how you experience your feelings. You may try to suppress them, for example, but strong feelings have a way of popping back up. It is usually possible, however, to control the public expression of your feelings. You may be furious at a colleague, for example, but you can learn how to control whether you rant and rave.

"Speech is such a huge part of our daily experience," says Joseph Goldstein, "and often its motive is to cause divisiveness or harm to others. But if we are willing to be open and honest about the mix of motivations behind our speech and our actions, then we can choose the motives which are most wholesome and act from those, and let the others go."[1]

Different situations appropriately call for different levels of self-disclosure. More often than not, it is prudent to prac-tice restraint and avoid public displays of your strongest feel-ings. Indeed, to indiscriminately express all your emotions could undermine your authority and effectiveness, not to mention upset your colleagues. This is particularly true in times of crisis, when people need leaders to display calm and a semblance of control. A good example comes from Katharine Graham, former publisher of the *Washington Post*, who in her Pulitzer Prize–winning autobiography describes her fears about a possible strike by the newspaper's unions: "I felt desperate and secretly wondered if I might have blown the whole thing and lost the paper. I didn't really see how we were going to manage. The only way I can describe the extent of my anxiety is to say that I felt as if I were pregnant with a rock. Yet, despite my inner turmoil, I had to appear calm and determined and to come across as optimistic in order to convey that attitude to others."[2]

Stories like Graham's propel seasoned leaders, in their quiet moments, to jokingly compare their life to that of a duck gliding across a pond. Above the water's surface, it's all grace, composure, and smooth sailing; underneath, it's nothing but frantic paddling to maintain momentum and direction and the pretense of being totally in control (which, of course, no one is).

Graham's observation also illustrates one of the most common ways of concealing discomfort—namely, using the mask of calm, confidence, and cheerfulness. You may be rattled by a sudden crisis, but if asked, you would definitely deny it. You may be drowning under the pressure of high expectations, but you certainly are not going to show it. Indeed, in her study of new managers, Linda Hill discovered that many were "reluctant to mention the extent of their upset, even to their spouses."[3]

As dean, I remember chairing a spring faculty meeting, which couldn't be postponed, while, outside, a group of angry students was demonstrating against what they saw as shortcomings in the school's process for hiring faculty of color. The students were chanting, playing drums, and blocking the street—all in an effort to be heard. Not knowing what to do and churning inside, I chaired the meeting with a strained smile and tried to act as if I were in control! A former principal calls this pattern "the art of the bluff." Looking back, I call it a missed opportunity to

E

listen and share my perspective and feelings with the faculty—
and with the students.

Indeed, it often makes sense to drop your mask at the office—
at least partly. Showing vulnerability, not having the answers,
and asking for help can all be signs of competence, not weakness.
For example, Barry Jentz and I have suggested that confusion
is widespread among leaders because it's often so hard to know
what's going on or what to do. We argue that leaders need to
own their confusion—and, instead of concealing it, open up to their
coworkers and clearly acknowledge the need to make sense of
the confusing situation: "[Acknowledging one's confusion] helps
others to do the same—to claim their own confusion and begin
trying to make sense out of a disorienting situation. By taking
the lead, you make it easier for others to follow."[4]

Handwritten notes of appreciation are another example of
dropping your mask (see chapter 9). Not only do they nourish
the writer, but even short notes of thanks can have a big impact
on staff members, who see a more human side of you: a boss
willing to pause, show gratitude, and take the time to do it by
hand. Indeed, I recently met with a school superintendent who
independently brought up the same topic. He regularly reminds
his principals that writing short handwritten notes of appreciation for specific actions taken was one of the most important
things the principals could do in building school morale—and
he reminded me that most educators have in their desks a drawer
where such treasured gifts are kept. Nourishing for you, and
wonderfully humanizing for the organization.

Still another example of dropping your mask comes from a
tale I was told while teaching at the University of Pennsylvania. A nearby network of school superintendents often privately
swapped stories about job hassles: the endless night meetings
filled with conflict, the unexpected crises, the stinging criticism
of their leadership. Near the end of an unusually frank discussion,
all eyes turned to an esteemed—and silent—superintendent.

Responding to his peers, he declared with bravado, "Hey, the hassles don't get to me—I sleep like a baby." Then, hesitantly, he dropped his mask of control and continued with a hitch in his voice: "I sometimes sleep for a few hours, and then I wake up crying. Just like the old joke says."

For sure, not every leader sheds tears over the pressures of leadership, but many leaders, even among the most competent and well adjusted, experience much emotional discomfort on the job. Indeed, we can almost feel the relief in a room of superintendents as a respected colleague breaks the taboo against self-disclosure by making himself or herself vulnerable. We can almost hear the other superintendents say to themselves, "You mean I'm not alone?"

This story has added value as a reminder that how and to whom you reveal your emotions can be crucial. In many cases, unmasking feelings only works in the presence of the right audience. For example, while I was dean, I once gave a speech to a group of donors and faculty members, and in my remarks, I likened fund-raising to building friendships. While telling stories about the generosity of several donors in the audience, I became visibly choked up. The donors, with whom I had developed strong bonds of trust, told me later that they were deeply moved by my remarks. In contrast, several worried faculty thought I had lost my marbles, misreading my tears as a sign of affliction, not affection. It was a reminder of both the benefits and the costs of displaying feelings in public.

NAMING YOUR FEELINGS

In dropping your mask, you not only need to be sensitive to who is in your audience, but also must be careful about how you make your feelings known. Indeed, there's a big difference between showing your emotions and naming them. Showing your emotions can scare your colleagues, making them think you no longer

E

have your hand on the wheel, and thus, such behavior can sometimes undermine trust in your leadership. In contrast, naming your feelings, without all the drama of acting out the emotions, can reassure others that you are a normal human being in contact with reality and in control of the situation. Naming is the sweet spot, a productive middle way between a restrained Mr. Spock and a reckless Captain Kirk.

For example, the superintendent in the earlier vignette neither remained aloof nor burst into tears; instead, he let people know some of the details of his sleepless nights. In your case, you can put a name to your pain, perhaps by saying something like this to your boss: "When you changed your decision after our meeting this morning, I felt angry because it weakened my relationship with my staff." Such a measured response—which is specific about the event, names your feeling, and cites the consequences for you—is much more effective than suppressing your feelings or impulsively venting your frustration and banging on the desk.

The following short exercise, "Name It!," is designed to help you learn how to express your feelings wisely by naming them instead of hiding them or acting out in some counterproductive way. Because we express ourselves with our gestures and facial expressions as well as our words, the exercise calls for the use of a mirror.

NAME IT! (10–15 minutes)

When you are ready, take a few moments to identify a work situation in which you are upset and feel the need to give a colleague negative feedback. For example, perhaps someone has talked behind your back in a destructive way and you feel livid.

If it's difficult to come up with a real-life example right now, here's an alternative: imagine a work situation that really makes you churn—with frustration, anxiety, disappointment, or whatever. Let's say the situation calls out for a face-to-face meeting with a colleague to clear the air.

Now, imagine a meeting where you intend to set forth your concern. Remember, the goal is to practice expressing your feelings wisely by naming them instead of showing them. Imagine what you would say and how you want to appear. For instance, you might calmly say something like this: "When you failed to attend the kickoff meeting last Tuesday, I was really disappointed because it undermined the solidarity we were trying to display," or "When I got your feedback on my performance yesterday, I felt quite upset because of all the negative comments."

When you are ready, practice before a mirror what you plan to say. Listen to how you sound, including your tone of voice. Notice how you look: your facial expressions, body movements, and small gestures. The aim is to be candid, calm, and in command of your emotions while being clear about how you feel. Practice until you are able to express your strong feelings without displaying them in an unproductive manner.

When you are ready, bring the exercise to an end with the intention of integrating this naming strategy into your interaction with others.

Not only do you need to name your feelings, but as a working professional, you also often need to offer a plan of action—a structure and a process—for moving beyond the situation. Here's an example that reflects work with my coach Barry Jentz.

Imagine that your weekly staff meeting is interrupted by your secretary, who reports an organizational flap. After he leaves, you might say something like this to your staff, which names your feeling and suggests an action plan: "I'm troubled about what we just heard, and I think it requires our attention today so that it

E

doesn't turn into a full-blown crisis. We have thirty minutes left in today's meeting. I'd suggest we spend fifteen minutes hearing your concerns and insights. Then, I'd like to spend a few minutes giving you my perspective. After that, let's talk about putting in place a process for moving forward. Who would like to begin?" By calmly naming your feelings—and establishing a structure for the meeting and a plan for the future—you are better able to express your feelings while maintaining your authority, and you can move forward in a systematic way.

To be sure, how you deliver your message—your tone, posture, gestures, sense of confidence—is just as important as your words. In our research on confusion, Jentz and I concluded that "unless you unambiguously assert, with conviction and without apology, your sense of being confused, others will fulfill your worst expectations—concluding that you *are* weak—and they will be less willing to engage in a shared process of interpersonal learning."[5]

EXPRESSING FEELINGS INDIRECTLY

In some organizations, any expression of feelings by the boss often just plain violates the norms. In these cases, you can show your human side indirectly, through what's sometimes called the *natural triad*.[6] We're all familiar with natural triads at home and at the office: for example, a loving mother of a sullen teenager asks a favorite aunt for help, or a beloved school secretary's job in part is to humanize an imposing principal to the school's teachers.

If you're in a position of authority, for example, you might ask a top assistant to genuinely befriend your staff and act as a two-way conduit of information. Unhappy staff members might be reluctant to confront the boss, so the theory goes, but they will raise concerns with the boss's confidant. In response, the confidant can put a human face on your upsetting behavior. Authentic go-betweens are vital to meeting a major problem faced by many organizations: getting crucial information from the bottom to the top. And they can help you express your feelings wisely, if not always directly.

DISPLAYING WARMTH

In dropping your mask, you also need to prudently reveal your warm feelings—even love—for your colleagues and your organization. But it's important to remember that the act and expression of caring will often make you feel—and look—vulnerable. After all, you can't genuinely care about your organization and colleagues without taking risks and thereby opening up to the possibility of being hurt and being criticized for being "soft." Care and vulnerability are two sides of the same coin.

Your feelings of caring can be expressed not only in words, but also in your day-to-day actions—in the priority you pay to listening and empathy, not to mention random acts of kindness and compassion. Empathy—the ability to put yourself in the shoes of another and test your sense of what the person is trying to express (e.g., "So, you're really hurt by what I did?")—is the key to helping others feel understood, cared for, and truly heard.

Your feelings are also expressed by sharing elation with workmates in moments of joy. You might share your delight in the birth of a baby, a promotion, or the completion of a project well done. Public praise and recognition can make a big difference. Moreover, in moments of personal need, words and deeds can offer comfort—for example, by visiting sick colleagues, by attending family funerals, or by just being there in moments of uncertainty. And if norms and circumstances permit, you can offer a warm touch or a gentle hug.

As I was writing this section, a conversation I had some twenty years ago came to mind. It was with the legendary dean of the Harvard Business School, John McArthur. As the newly appointed dean of the Harvard Graduate School of Education,

E

I trekked across the Charles River to seek advice from John, a no-nonsense, experienced manager. Sitting on a plush sofa sipping herbal tea in the Dean's House, I asked John to identify the most important thing I needed to do as a new dean, expecting a hard-headed answer about the centrality of careful analysis.

John leaned back, thought for a moment, and said, "You need to make house calls." Dumbfounded, I asked him to elaborate. I needed to reach out and listen to my tenured colleagues, he said, one by one, and on their own turf, when they were most in need. His way was to visit their houses and sit around their kitchen tables, often with a bottle of wine, and just listen to what was troubling them. It was good advice from a wise, tough-minded man who, of course, knew the importance of analysis and who, beneath an often gruff exterior, understood the centrality of being empathetic and showing his humanity.

Sometimes, the best way to express your caring is by not saying a word. Not offering advice. Not offering reassurance. Not trying to fix anything. In fact, sometimes, you help by not doing anything. Other than showing up with all your heart and silently holding a space for a colleague in need. Perhaps even by holding the person in your arms, just as Chris Germer did for me, as described earlier.

Matt Licata and Jeff Foster beautifully capture in a blog—poetry, really—the essence of what it means to show up and create a space that holds others and allows them to heal themselves.

> *When you sit with a friend in pain,*
> *when their world no longer makes sense;*
> *when confusion rages and*
> *no rest is to be found.*
> *Just for a moment,*
> *will you resist the temptation*
> *to make things better,*
> *to reassure them,*

to provide answers,
even to heal them?
Will you offer your stillness, your listening,
your presence, and the warmth
of your immediacy?
Will you hold them in your heart,
with the same tenderness
of a mother holding her little one?
Will you embrace them where they are,
without needing them to change or transform
according to your own needs and schedule?
Will you stay close,
holding your own impatience
and discomfort near?
Will you look into their eyes
and see yourself?
Will you stay in the inferno of healing
with them, trusting in disintegration,
knowing that you are only witnessing
the falling away of an old dream?
Sometimes in doing nothing
everything is undone,
and love is revealed to be
the only true medicine.[7]

HANDLING THE UNEXPECTED

It's one thing to express your feelings wisely at work when things are going smoothly. It's quite another when you are faced with unsettling events that are totally unexpected. You can easily lose your bearings, jump to conclusions, and act precipitously, saying and doing things you later regret.

Such reactive behavior comes almost automatically, especially when you thoughtfully extend yourself to another, only to feel

E

rejected or attacked in return. In such situations, the reflexive response is to feel hurt and respond in kind. "If you attack me," you say to yourself subconsciously, "I'll attack you in return." The following parable, based on my readings, emphasizes how the reactive response might not always be appropriate.

There was a young man hiking in the woods, enjoying the beautiful fall foliage. As he climbed over a hill, he saw a small dog standing still, knee deep in leaves. As the hiker warily approached the hungry-looking animal, he noticed that the dog did not move. Walking slowly, the hiker took off his knapsack, removed a bag of trail mix, and extended a handful to the dog—who immediately bit his hand. Startled by the dog's response to his good deed, the furious hiker started looking for a stick to strike back—until he noticed that the dog's front left leg was caught in a trap beneath the leaves.

In our work, it is not unusual to be thrown by what Jentz and I call *oh-no moments*—unexpected events that cause our minds to race and our emotions to churn, often resulting in intemperate reactions, as almost happened in the dog parable. Sometimes, we can be thrown by an unforeseen policy shift or crisis. Other times, we can become bent out of shape by an annoying event—for example, a colleague who continually interrupts at meetings. Still other times, unhelpful thoughts will just pop into our heads—for example, "I just can't handle all the pressure." In all these situations, it is easy to become frazzled and say—and do—something stupid.

Instead of reacting impulsively and rashly, you can, with the help of the following two exercises, respond to unexpected events by pausing to gather and ground yourself, and then express your feelings and take action deliberately and wisely.

The first exercise, "Morning ABCs," focuses on awareness, breathing, and compassion (your ABCs) and, if you are inclined, direction. The meditation combines several of the MY DANCE steps we've explored so far. You can use it as a calming morning check-in to gauge where you are and to set the stage for a good day. Equally important, you can use it on the spot to help navigate disorienting events.

This practice can help anchor you in the here and now, smooth out your waves of emotions, provide a breathing space to make wiser choices, and prepare you to act—not just react—calmly, clearly, and with a sense of direction. Through the exercise, you practice expressing your human side without going overboard.

MORNING ABCs   (5–10 minutes)

When you are ready, direct your attention to the following steps.

1. *Awareness:* Start by checking your internal weather, that is, what's going on inside you right now. Ask yourself, "What's my emotional temperature right now? What am I thinking about in this moment? What bodily sensations am I experiencing here and now?" You're not trying to fix anything or push anything away. Just make room for what's here, acknowledge it, and allow it to be. You might silently say something like this: "I notice something in me that's furious with the school board. I'm going to allow my anger to be just as it is." For a moment more, continue to notice, acknowledge, and be with your here–and–now experiences, watching them as they come and go.

2. *Breathing:* When it feels right, shift your attention to your breath. Breathe in . . . breathe out. You might choose to narrow your attention to the rising and falling of your belly as you breathe in . . . breathe out. Allow your breath to establish its own soothing rhythm. When your mind wanders, gently bring your attention back to your breath. Back to your belly. For a moment more, continue breathing in . . . breathing out.

E

207

3. *Compassion:* Now, shift your attention to how you are treating yourself right now. Take a moment to ask, "Am I giving myself a hard time?" If you are being self-critical, consider treating yourself with the kindness and understanding that you would show a dear friend. You might silently say something like this: "Yeah, I screwed up with the school board, but I'm only human," or "This is a really tough situation I face—no wonder it makes me nervous." You might also place a soothing hand on the spot that aches the most in your body. For a moment more, just be with your pain, and give yourself this gift of self-compassion.

4. *Direction:* When we struggle with difficult moments, it's easy to lose our sense of direction. So, take a moment to recall what you truly value—for example, respect for your colleagues, careful listening, fair and firm action. Indeed, ask yourself, "What matters most to me?" After that, take another moment to envision *action* guided by these core values. Ask yourself, "How can I move toward what I stand for, rather than escape my discomfort?" You might silently say something like this: "I'm going to speak my mind at today's board meeting—despite my fears—because I truly value open communication." And for a moment more, take pride in your courage and commitment.

Finally, thank your body and mind for all its hard work, open your eyes if they had been closed, and return to your day ahead with the intention of bringing a new sense of centeredness to your words and actions.

Sometimes we're thrown by unexpected events, and in that moment, it feels like an emotional emergency. The following exercise, which resembles "Morning ABCs," is intended to provide emotional first aid. "SOS Full Stop" helps you calm the fire in your heart, ground yourself in your experiences, and prepare yourself to interact with others wisely despite your strong feelings. The exercise calls for you to stand up, open up, and show up (SOS), and it combines elements from other meditations described above. Symbolically, the exercise suggests that in emergency-like situations, we make a full stop and stand up to reality and respond prudently, rather than be flattened by events and become a slave to our emotions. See how this exercise works for you; it can be done relatively quickly.

SOS FULL STOP   (3–5 minutes)

Practice these three steps before you encounter an emotional emergency so that when one does arise, you will feel more prepared.

1. *Stand up "solefully"*: Start by bringing your attention to the soles of your feet, as if your mind were a powerful flashlight that you can control. Concentrate your mind on the experience of your feet touching the floor. If you can, let all your weight fall through your body, through the soles of your feet into the floor, as if you were rooted in mother earth. No need to fix anything. No need to judge anything. No need to do anything special. When your mind wanders, say to yourself, "No problem," and just keep bringing your attention back to the sensations of your feet on the ground. Notice how you feel connected, grounded, anchored to the earth.

2. *Open up:* When you are ready, broaden the focus of your mind's flashlight to a wide-angle lens. For a moment, open up and observe your emotional weather. Ask yourself, "How am I feeling right now? What thoughts are racing through my mind? What body sensations are prominent? What's my mood right now?" No need to fix anything. Just observe your internal weather, and let it be as it is. For a moment more, just stay with your difficult stuff, letting it come and letting it go.

E

> **3.** *Show up:* When you are ready, now shift your attention from your emotional weather to dealing with what feels like an emergency. Ask yourself, "Which parts of me are likely to show up in this troubling situation? My stressed self? My entangled self? My reactive self?" Instead, imagine showing up as the part of your mind—your Light—that can step back and just notice your unexpected turmoil, instead of getting swept away by it. The part of your mind that's grounded and aware and witnesses your turmoil from a broad perspective. Now, imagine resting in this broad perspective as you turn toward the apparent emergency you face.
>
> Finally, thank your body and mind for all its hard work, open your eyes, and return to your day ahead with the intention of bringing this broad perspective to your work.

On the whole, many of us are often quite wary about revealing our human side at work—and there are good reasons for our reluctance: disclosure often violates norms; there are few guideposts as to when, where, and how to reveal our feelings; and, surely, openness is sometimes counterproductive. Not to mention the risks of literally extending a gentle hand in a workplace that's appropriately sensitive about the boundaries of sexual harassment.

Nonetheless, education leaders should experiment with being more open about their vulnerabilities and feelings, being themselves, warts and all—and even occasionally showing tears of sorrow or righteous anger. "Real dishes break," says writer Marty Rubin. "That's how you know they're real." Leaders should also pay special attention to empathy and caring for their colleagues, for it's easy to underestimate the importance of setting a warm and genuine tone. In many cases, your disarming honesty and displays of compassion can promote stronger connections built on caring and trust, can lead to better problem solving, and can help create an energizing sense of common humanity—the sense that we are all in this together.

REMEMBER TO BE A GIRAFFE

In concluding this discussion of the final step of MY DANCE, I'd like to share a poem that sums up several of the main points made along the way. The poem—a Jerry Murphy original—is about giraffes, one of my favorite animals. To set the scene for the poem, I offer some observations about the giraffe:

- The giraffe is the tallest mammal on earth. It dreams about reaching far-off water holes that no other animal can even see.
- The giraffe is the creature with the longest neck. The animal dances from one acacia tree to another, eating the highest leaves and undeterred by the thorns and rain.
- Giraffes are amazingly resilient. When a calf is born, it drops six feet to the ground. From day one, it learns to accept the hardships of life—and to rise undaunted after a breathtaking fall.
- Each giraffe is a beautiful, unique creature—one of a kind. No two giraffes have the same spots.
- The giraffe is blessed with a huge heart—indeed, the biggest heart that walks the earth.

So, how does all this relate to leadership? Well, in today's demanding times, it's not enough to be a strong leader, tough as nails. You must also . . .

E

REMEMBER TO BE A GIRAFFE

Live your dreams while standing tall
Stick your neck out on hearing your call
Rise undeterred whenever you fall
Prize your special gifts on the long haul
Open your big heart to yourself and to all
And dance wholeheartedly in every squall

Yes, leadership promises a rainy path
and also
The chance to serve—and even laugh
If you just remember to be a giraffe

Putting It All Together

Pick Up Your Feet and Dance

Tell me, what is it you plan to do with
your one wild and precious life?

—*Mary Oliver*

SO, THERE YOU HAVE IT: MY DANCE, step by step. I hope you
share my enthusiasm for this enterprise. I believe these steps can
help transform your leadership and life. But some of you may
still need a tad more convincing—after all, learning these steps
is a lot of work, especially since they call for action that may
be the exact opposite of how you currently handle difficulties at
work. So, I'd like to conclude by pulling together the main reasons why MY DANCE is an excellent investment for stressed education leaders "up to their ass in alligators." After that, I'll suggest
two specific, practical tools you can use to help turn MY DANCE
into action. And then I'll end by inviting you to pick up your
feet—literally—and dance in the inescapable rain of leadership
and life, even if you hate to dance!

WHY *MY DANCE*?

You may have heard the story of Dan Harris, coanchor of *Night-line* and the weekend editions of *Good Morning America*. After suffering a panic attack on live television, Harris turned to meditation with great skepticism, but then went on to recount (with humorous irreverence) what he had discovered about his own self-growth in his down-to-earth, best-selling book, *10% Happier*.[1] Like me, you may be motivated to learn more about mindfulness because you are inspired by the personal transformations of individuals like Harris. Or perhaps you're willing to put in the time and effort because you have come to recognize that your reliance on the three Rs—resistance, rumination, and self-rebuke—often makes difficult situations quite unbearable. Or perhaps you're simply dissatisfied with a life where you are doing your best to survive and keep your head above the water, and you recognize that this way of life is a far cry from how you want to live. Or you may be eager to learn the steps of MY DANCE because you are drawn to the benefits of this approach to flourishing.

Let me recap these benefits here, but this time in more colloquial terms. The seven steps can help you let go, show up, and get moving on what really matters to you. With practice, you can learn to do the following:

- Let *go* of your unhelpful struggles with discomfort by allowing your upsets to be just as they are, even if they are highly unpleasant.
- Let *go* of the powerful urge to control what cannot be controlled—namely, your stressful thoughts and feelings, the behavior of others, how they respond to your best efforts, and what people think of you, not to mention your unique history and genes.
- Show up as your Light, with a wide perspective that allows you to watch your troubles come and go instead of being overwhelmed by them.

- *Show up* for others, ready to work with colleagues and stake-holders with presence, concentration, and compassion—and with your core values front and center.
- *Get moving* toward a life of purpose, meaning, and vitality, with the wisdom, steadiness, and resiliency required to lead effectively, especially when you are experiencing intense discomfort.
- *Get moving* in areas where you can exercise considerable control—namely, where you place your attention, your behavior in pursuit of what matters most to you, the wise expression of your feelings at work, and your destiny as a leader.

You may be keen to learn this new approach for still another reason—because you have pondered the six weighty questions in the table presented shortly, and you are drawn to the answers offered by MY DANCE. For all these reasons, I invite you—even beseech you—to let go, show up, and get moving on MY DANCE.

DEVELOPING A PLAN

As you move forward, it's important to engage intellectually with the ideas embedded in MY DANCE. Even more important, however, is developing the skills to put the ideas into action. As I've emphasized earlier, the process is like learning to swim. You cannot make much progress by just discussing various strokes on the edge of the pool; you have to jump in and engage in specific exercises. For this reason, I've suggested mental workouts that might consist of activities you've chosen partly from the numerous exercises presented throughout this book.

But which exercises should make up the elements of your daily mental workout? One way to choose is to approach the task systematically, deciding which combination of exercises meets your needs and purposes. This planning approach would entail doing a self-assessment, establishing priorities, choosing exercises that are truly doable. Even if detailed planning is not your

Six important questions for leaders in education: Different approaches yield different answers

Question	"Fix-the-problem" approach	MY DANCE approach
What does discomfort mean to me?	A sign that something is wrong with me—I am a weak leader unable to handle difficult thoughts and emotions.	A sign that something is right with me—I am a real person who is aware that there is no leading without bleeding.
How do I handle discomfort when it shows up?	Respond with three Rs: *resist* discomfort, *ruminate* over it, and *rebuke* myself for not measuring up.	Allow discomfort to be just as it is, stay with it in the present moment, and show compassion for myself and others.
Each day, where do I place my attention?	I'll gain the most by focusing on trying to get rid of discomfort.	I'll gain the most by focusing on the here and now and on my core values—and use discomfort as my teacher.
Each day, which part of me shows up at work?	My reactive self, which aims to escape from or avoid discomfort.	I show up as my Light, a part of me that illuminates and makes room for upsets and takes them less personally.
What guides my leadership journey?	My level of discomfort, social rules, and what others expect.	My core values—the qualities and ideals that matter most to me.
How do I act in risky, high-stakes situations?	Avoid actions that trigger discomfort or disapproval, and let others take the lead.	Take prudent actions that express my values, even when these actions trigger upsetting emotions in me.

Source: Inspired by Kirk Strosahl, Patricia Robinson, and Thomas Gustavsson, *Brief Interventions for Radical Change: Principles and Practices of Focused Acceptance and Commitment Therapy* (Oakland, CA: New Harbinger, 2012).

favorite pastime, I encourage you to take a moment to see what such planning might look like and ponder whether it makes sense for you in real life.

Needs and Priorities

In essence, MY DANCE seeks to identify a to-do list aimed at living a meaningful and productive life in these stressful times. In fact, the seven steps can be boiled down to a short list of three imperatives:

- Spotlight *what matters* to you by clarifying your values and identifying values-inspired action.
- Take care of your *inner life* by detecting and disrupting the three Rs and by making time for nourishing activities.
- Take skillful *action* by expressing your feelings wisely as you put your values into action.

In choosing how to spend your practice time, you might start with a rough-and-ready assessment of where you stand on these imperatives by applying what I call the *fiddler crab test*. As you may know, the male fiddler crab is a tiny seaside critter with one really big claw and a much smaller claw. You might ask yourself, "Which of these three imperatives, if any, is already a big claw for me? That is, which imperative is strong and well developed and thus requires less attention? Which is my least-developed, small claw—the imperative that requires my top priority?"

In doing your assessment, you might say something like this to yourself: "I think I'm pretty good at putting my values into action; that's my big claw. What gets in the way is being ham-fisted when it comes to taking care of myself, mostly because I spend so much time ruminating and beating myself up, which just makes my life miserable. That's my small claw, but it also spills over into my behavior in public, where I often act precipitously and lash out when I'm under a lot of pressure. This tendency undermines my efforts to do what matters."

In establishing priorities, you might say something like this to yourself: "I'm really busy the next month, so the best I can do is set aside just a few moments every morning—even that will be a stretch. I think I'll start by focusing my attention on disrupting my rumination and self-rebuke. Next month, when my schedule lightens up, I plan to build more healing activities into my day and to work on my tendency to overreact when I'm really upset."

Action Steps

Ideally, your plan would contain the specifics of what you are going to do: when, where, how often, and roughly for what length of time. You might find it helpful to write down your plan, which could look something like this:

> Early each morning for the next month, I'll set aside fifteen minutes for a daily mental workout. After taking a moment to settle in, I'll turn to my two top priorities this month.
>
> First, I want to address my incessant ruminating. So for my workout, I'll do a guided breathing meditation for about ten minutes, which will help sharpen my capacity to detect rumination and divert my attention away from it. My second priority is addressing my habit of rebuking myself. So, I plan to practice the "Soften, Soothe, Allow" exercise, which should take about five minutes.
>
> During the rest of the day, I plan to pause three or more times to focus on the present moment. I might take a few deep breaths or focus on sounds to be heard. To remind myself to pause during the day, I'll set my computer to ring a mindfulness bell every few hours.
>
> After implementing this plan for a month, I'll take stock and perhaps develop a new plan that targets other

priorities—for example, making more space for nourishing activities.

You might commit to such a plan because you believe that daily practice, aimed specifically at the priorities you've identified, can help train your mind and open your heart.

REMEMBERING LISTS

You might devise a plan, as suggested above, or you might find it helpful to follow a different yet complementary approach— namely, relying on written reminders to help set your daily path and to remind yourself of practices that are helpful to you. I keep my lists on my smartphone for convenience and portability. To give you the flavor of what I do, here's the list I call my *wake-up menu*, which I use to start my day. I begin by deliberately making and drinking my espresso in a way that turns the actions into a "Five-Sense Pause." After that, I choose from other "Starters" (warm-up activities) and "House Specials" (extended exercises). Except for "Reviewing MY DANCE," which refers to the seven steps of MY DANCE summarized in chapter 3, each item in the list refers to a practice described in the book.

WAKE-UP MENU

Starters	*House Specials*
Five-Sense Pause	Mindful Breathing
Morning ABCs	Warm Wishes
Reviewing MY DANCE	Soften, Soothe, Allow
Seven Top Values	CVS Morning Pause

Lists like these jog my memory when I want to do a particular meditation. They help me recall what I stand for. They provide food for thought and for action—and for inspiration. If this idea appeals to you, you might give it a try, coming up with lists that work for you and putting them on your smartphone, another device, or index cards.

ONWARD AND UPWARD

I hope I have heightened your enthusiasm for learning how to put the seven steps of MY DANCE into action. They reflect a growing body of scientific evidence that documents the benefits of training the mind. These steps have made a huge difference in my daily life—both professionally and personally. I fervently hope they can do the same for you.

MY DANCE offers a practical and hopeful antidote to the relentless pressures of leadership, education, or life itself. It is not a quick fix, but with perseverance, patience, and practice, you can learn to abandon the quixotic quest to eliminate stress by trying to fix yourself. Paradoxical as it may sound, by making space for your difficulties, you are choosing a path away from being a victim of circumstances in today's frenzied world.

Even more important, you are choosing a path toward flourishing as a leader in education. Indeed, this book is really about flourishing in the midst of the rain that professional life brings, by

- seeking what matters most to you with tenacity, courage, and humility;
- opening your heart and mind, and choosing to welcome life's ups and downs;
- getting out of your own way and learning to live in your own skin; and
- being a genuine and compassionate human being in your dealings with others.

In keeping with this focus on flourishing, I'll conclude with a story and a final exercise. Both capture the essence of dancing in the rain and staying fully alive even in the face of life's inevitable storms. The story describes a wife's first experiences at the Mayo Clinic as she accompanied her husband for evaluation of his earlier diagnosis of Lou Gehrig's disease:

> We heard a pianist playing somewhere nearby . . . [in] the stunning Atrium . . . It was crowded at the time, filled with folks who had stopped to listen to two women, one playing the piano and one singing . . . It was the first song we had ever danced to and the song we had danced to at our wedding, nine years and one month to the day before.
>
> Randall put down his briefcase filled with doctors reports and test results, took me in his arms, and danced me all over that floor. I have to say, it was glorious! I only had eyes for him, but when it was over and folks were applauding, we became acutely aware of how many people gathered around were in wheelchairs or were with those who were.
>
> We suddenly realized that in that spontaneous moment of celebration, we had been dancing on behalf of the life and love that lived in each person gathered together in that place. It was one of many moments today in which we experienced the tender unity of vulnerability.
>
> From the moment we walked through the entry, lined with hundreds of waiting wheelchairs, we found ourselves thinking of the Pool of Bethesda . . . We imagined Jesus asking us that essential question: "Do you want to be healed?" . . . We thought we might have heard him say, "Then pick up your feet and dance."[2]

Pick up your feet and dance, indeed. In this wholehearted spirit, I invite you to engage in "Rockin' with Elvis," one final exercise that can get your heart beating and your blood flowing. I've used this activity in my teaching at Harvard, and many students describe it as an uplifting way to end an extended examination of MY DANCE.

As detailed below, I invite you to bring your attention to some discomfort you are experiencing in your professional life and, at the same time, dance to the sounds of Elvis Presley's "Jailhouse Rock." (Dancing is intended to illustrate what it's like to live life fully. Even if you dislike dancing, you may find the exercise valuable.) I've chosen this final exercise because it epitomizes what this book is all about—living an "and also" life. You can feel drenched by the rain *and also* get up and dance. I've chosen this song because we can think about MY DANCE as a way to escape the jail created by our self-defeating habits, to liberate ourselves from the shackles that have imprisoned us. So here we go, with one last exercise.

ROCKIN' WITH ELVIS *(5–10 minutes)*

Start by taking a minute or two to look inside and identify some difficult emotions that grow out of the rain of your life as a leader. You may feel distressed about a classroom's recent test results, an upcoming PTA meeting, the lack of appreciation for the stellar new principals hired, staff cuts for next year, and so on.

Now, identify a troubling emotion that's dominant in your consciousness at this moment. It need not be what's bugging you the most. In fact, it may be your fear of looking like a fool if you get up and dance.

When you're ready, take a few minutes more to just be with this discomfort. Not resisting it. Not ruminating over it. Not rebuking yourself for feeling what you feel. Just making space for the discomfort as you watch it come and go. You might say to yourself something like this: "I notice something in me that's very sad" and give the part of you that hurts a gentle hello and a touch of self-compassion.

Next, at the same time you are experiencing your troubling feelings, shift your focus to taking action consistent with what makes you come fully alive. For example, perhaps you are feeling hurt, disappointed, or worried. Instead of sitting there and ruminating on these feelings indefinitely, you might consider doing the opposite: stand up and dance. (If dancing doesn't make you feel fully alive, you might imagine a different activity that does. When feeling low, for example, you might imagine hiking in the mountains. At the very least, you might just consider bobbing up and down to the beat of the song!)

To set the scene, I invite you to find the song "Jailhouse Rock" sung by Elvis Presley on one of your devices. (One easy way is to search online for "Jailhouse Rock audio.") When you're ready, play the music.

Now, with the music blaring and you feeling the steady beat, see if you can let your hair down for a moment and get out of your own way. Stand up and rock. As you do so, be aware of the experience of both *feeling* difficult emotions and *doing* what matters to you in the moment.

This exercise provides a visceral sense of what's possible for you as a leader, an educator, a professional, and a human being. You are free from the need to be free from discomfort, and with a clear sense of what matters to you, you can learn to dance in the rain with a liberated mind, a glad heart, and an exuberant spirit. MY DANCE is really about becoming fully alive at work and in life.

Guide to
MY DANCE
Exercises

FURTHER READING AND OTHER RESOURCES

IN RECENT YEARS, the resources addressing the inner skills of students and teachers have grown significantly, while specific attention to the inner skills of education leaders is just beginning to take off (as exemplified in *The Mindful School Leader*, by Valerie Brown and Kirsten Olson). Still, an amazing array of relevant, insightful, and useful resources is readily available to education leaders. Here's an eclectic list of some of my favorites: a dozen books, a dozen websites, and a pertinent film that will also make you smile.

Books

Ezra Bayda, with Josh Bartok. *Saying Yes to Life (Even the Hard Parts)*. Boston: Wisdom Publications, 2005.
A lovely collection of discerning and inspiring aphorisms.

Pema Chödrön. *Taking the Leap: Freeing Ourselves from Old Habits and Fears*. Boston: Shambhala, 2009.
An illuminating volume, one of many, written by a beloved Buddhist nun.

Christopher K. Germer. *The Mindful Path to Self-Compassion: Freeing Yourself from Destructive Thoughts and Emotions*. New York: Guilford, 2009.
A secret sauce for living life fully; written with eloquence.

Joseph Goldstein. *Mindfulness: A Practical Guide to Awakening*. Boulder, CO: Sounds True, 2013.
A masterful look at mindfulness; written by a wise teacher and scholar.

Rick Hanson. *Hardwiring Happiness: The New Brain Science of Contentment, Calm, and Confidence*. New York: Harmony, 2013.
Mind-changing tips on becoming Teflon for the negative and Velcro for the positive.

Steven C. Hayes, with Spencer Smith. *Get Out of Your Mind and Into Your Life: The New Acceptance & Commitment Therapy*. Oakland, CA: New Harbinger, 2005.
Self-help to stop overthinking and start living; written by the father of ACT.

Sam M. Intrator and Megan Scribner, eds. *Leading from Within: Poetry That Sustains the Courage to Lead*. San Francisco: Jossey-Bass, 2007.
Memorable words that lift the hearts and souls of leaders.

Jon Kabat-Zinn. *Mindfulness for Beginners: Reclaiming the Present Moment—and Your Life*. Boulder, CO: Sounds True, 2012.
A short-and-sweet starter written by a maestro, with a CD of guided meditations.

Matthieu Ricard. *Why Meditate? Working with Thoughts and Emotions*. Translated by Sherab Chödzin. Carlsbad, CA: Hay House, 2010.
An antidote for skeptics; written by a brilliant Buddhist, with a CD of his thoughts.

David I. Rome. *Your Body Knows the Answer: Using Your FELT SENSE to Solve Problems, Effect Change & Liberate Creativity*. Boston: Shambhala, 2014.
A welcome—and propitious—union of mindfulness and focusing.

Sharon Salzberg. *Lovingkindness: The Revolutionary Art of Happiness*. Boston: Shambhala, 2004.
A classic that opens our minds and hearts; written by a revered Buddhist practitioner.

John Teasdale, Mark Williams, and Zindel Segal. *The Mindful Way Workbook: An 8-Week Program to Free Yourself from Depression and Emotional Distress*. New York: Guilford, 2014.
A self-help guide penned by eminent psychologists, with a CD of guided meditations.

Websites

ACT Mindfully: www.actmindfully.com.au
   Home of Russ Harris, a leading trainer for acceptance and commitment therapy (ACT).

Center for Contemplative Mind in Society: www.contemplativemind.org
   Fostering contemplative practices in higher education, in service of a more just world.

Center for Healthy Minds: www.centerhealthyminds.org
   Researching the mind to cultivate well-being and relieve suffering.

Center for Mindfulness: www.umassmed.edu/cfm
   Home of the acclaimed mindfulness-based stress reduction (MBSR) program.

Center for Mindful Self-Compassion: www.centerformsc.org
   Go-to site for learning and teaching mindful self-compassion.

Focusing Resources: www.focusingresources.com/?portfolio=get-bigger-than-whats-bugging-you
   A treasure trove on what focusing is and how it works; includes an edifying e-course.

Greater Good Science Center: www.greatergood.berkeley.edu
   Linking science with skills to foster a thriving, resilient, and compassionate society.

Mindful: www.mindful.org
   A lively new magazine helping to bring mindfulness practices into the mainstream.

Mindful Schools: www.mindfulschools.org
   Innovative online courses for developing mindful students, teachers, and leaders.

Mindfulness in Education Network: www.mindfuled.org
   Passionate educators working together to blend contemplative practices and schooling.

New Harbinger Publications: www.newharbinger.com
   Evidence-based books on mental health and more; includes self-help guides galore.

Sounds True Publishing: www.soundstrue.com
   A source of spirited books, guided meditations, and recorded thoughts of leading lights.

Movie

Inside Out. Directed and cowritten by Pete Docter; codirected and cowritten by Ronnie del Carmen. Pixar Animation Studios and Walt Disney Pictures, 2015.

A mind-blowing emotion picture for kids—and education leaders too. For a trailer, see www.youtube.com/watch?v=seMwpP0yeu4.

POSTLUDE

IN HER BOOK *The Dance*, author Oriah Mountain Dreamer asks the questions that we can all ask ourselves as we begin our dance in the rain:

> What if there is no need to change, no need to try to transform yourself into someone who is more compassionate, more present, more loving or wise?
>
> How would this affect all the places in your life where you are endlessly trying to be better?
>
> What if the task is simply to unfold, to become who you already are in your essential nature — gentle, compassionate, and capable of living fully and passionately present?
>
> How would this affect how you feel when you wake up in the morning? . . .
>
> What if the question is not why am I so infrequently the person I really want to be, but why do I so infrequently want to be the person I really am?
>
> How would this change what you think you have to learn?
>
> What if becoming who and what we truly are happens not through striving and trying but by recognizing and receiving the people and places and practices that offer us the warmth of encouragement we need to unfold?

How would this shape the choices you make about how to spend today?

What if you knew that the impulse to move in a way that creates beauty in the world will arise from deep within and guide you every time you simply pay attention and wait?

How would this shape your stillness, your movement, your willingness to follow this impulse, to just let go and dance?[1]

NOTES

Introduction

1. Metropolitan Life Insurance Company, "The MetLife Survey of the American Teacher: Challenges for School Leadership," February 21, 2013, www.metlife.com/about/press-room/index.html?compID= 93364.

2. *Wikipedia*, s.v. "Yerkes-Dodson law," last modified May 30, 2015, https://en.wikipedia.org/wiki/Yerkes%E2%80%93Dodson_law.

3. This book builds on, and borrows from, several of my earlier writings: Jerome T. Murphy, "The Unheroic Side of Leadership: Notes from the Swamp," *Phi Delta Kappan* 69, no. 9 (May 1988): 654–659; Jerome T. Murphy, "Embracing the Enemy," in *Out-of-the-Box Leadership*, ed. Paul D. Houston et al. (Thousand Oaks, CA: Corwin, 2007), 133–153; and Jerome T. Murphy, "Dancing in the Rain: Tips on Thriving as a Leader in Tough Times," *Phi Delta Kappan* 93, no. 1 (September 2011): 36–41.

4. Dan Edwards et al., "The Activist's Ally: Contemplative Tools for Social Change" (Northampton, MA: Center for Contemplative Mind in Society, 2007, 2011), www.contemplativemind.org/admin/ wp-content/uploads/2012/09/Ally-sample.pdf.

5. Donald Jay Rothberg, *The Engaged Spiritual Life: A Buddhist Approach to Transforming Ourselves and the World* (Boston: Beacon, 2006), 93.

6. Matthieu Ricard, *Why Meditate?*, trans. Sherab Chödzin Kohn (Carlsbad, CA: Hay House, 2010), 12.

7. For example, see Valerie Brown and Kirsten Olson, *The Mindful School Leader: Practices to Transform Your Leadership and School* (Thousand Oaks, CA: Corwin, 2015).

8. Jon Kabat-Zinn, *Mindfulness for Beginners: Reclaiming the Present Moment—and Your Life* (Boulder, CO: Sounds True, 2012), 1.

9. Matthieu Ricard, Antoine Lutz, and Richard J. Davidson, "Mind of the Meditator," *Scientific American* 311, no. 5 (November 2014): 40–42.

Chapter 1

1. Mark Epstein, *The Trauma of Everyday Life* (New York: Penguin, 2013), 3.
2. Jennifer Cheatham, in "Everybody's Talking About Equity, but Nobody Knows the Meaning of the Word," Askwith Forum, Harvard Graduate School of Education, October 30, 2015.
3. Linda A. Hill, *Becoming a Manager: How New Managers Master the Challenges of Leadership* (Boston: Harvard Business Review Press, 2003), 175.
4. Ibid., 182.
5. Rick Ginsberg, "Being Boss Is Hard: The Emotional Side of Being in Charge," *Phi Delta Kappan* 90, no. 4 (December 2008): 292–297.
6. Jerome T. Murphy, *State Leadership in Education: On Being a Chief State School Officer* (Washington, DC: Institute for Educational Leadership, 1980), 111.
7. Ronald A. Heifetz and Marty Linsky, "A Survival Guide for Leaders," *Harvard Business Review* 80, no. 6 (June 2002): 65–74.
8. Richard H. Ackerman and Pat Maslin-Ostrowski, *The Wounded Leader: How Real Leadership Emerges in Times of Crisis* (San Francisco: Jossey-Bass, 2002), xii.
9. Heifetz and Linsky, "Survival Guide," 65–74.
10. Mary Grassa O'Neill, "How Do We Keep Good Principals?" commentary, *Education Week* 35, no. 12 (November 11, 2015): 28.

Chapter 2

1. This pressure to hide our feelings and be positive is beautifully illustrated in the 2016 Oscar-winning film *Inside Out*.
2. George H. Eifert and John P. Forsyth, *Acceptance & Commitment Therapy for Anxiety Disorders: A Practitioner's Treatment Guide to Use Mindfulness, Acceptance, and Values-Based Behavior Change Strategies* (Oakland, CA: New Harbinger, 2005), 63.
3. This statement was made by Siegel in a no-longer-available video presentation for an online course through the National Institute for the Clinical Application of Behavioral Medicine.
4. These examples are adapted from Ruth Baer, *The Practicing Happiness Workbook: How Mindfulness Can Free You from the 4 Psychological Traps That Keep You Stressed, Anxious, and Depressed* (Oakland, CA: New Harbinger, 2014), 25–26.
5. Jeffrey Young (superintendent of schools, Cambridge, Massachusetts), interview with author, October 26, 2015.

6. Jack Kornfield, *The Wise Heart: A Guide to the Universal Teachings of Buddhist Psychology* (New York: Bantam, 2008), 139.

7. Ibid., 139.

8. Matthew McKay and Catharine Sutker, *Leave Your Mind Behind: The Everyday Practice of Finding Stillness amid Rushing Thoughts* (Oakland, CA: New Harbinger, 2007), 4.

9. Christopher K. Germer, *The Mindful Path to Self-Compassion: Freeing Yourself from Destructive Thoughts and Emotions* (New York: Guilford, 2009), 1.

10. These examples are from Baer, *Happiness Workbook*, 69.

11. Sylvia Boorstein, *Don't Just Do Something, Sit There* (New York: Harper Collins, 1996), 59.

12. Joel Guarna, "New Harbinger's Interview with Steve Hayes," *Association for Contextual Behavioral Science*, accessed December 14, 2015, https://contextualscience.org/new_harbingers_interview_with_steve_hayes.

13. A variant of this equation, Pain × Resistance = Suffering, is found widely in the literature. For example, see Germer, *The Mindful Path*, 15.

14. Robert M. Sapolsky, *Why Zebras Don't Get Ulcers: The Acclaimed Guide to Stress, Stress-Related Diseases, and Coping* (New York: Macmillan, 2004), 384.

Chapter 3

1. Goodreads, s.v. "Oliver Wendell Holmes Sr.," accessed December 14, 2015, www.goodreads.com/quotes/44564-for-the-simplicity-on-this-side-of-complexity-i-wouldn-t.

2. Jerome T. Murphy, "Embracing the Enemy," in *Out-of-the-Box Leadership*, ed. Paul D. Houston et al. (Thousand Oaks, CA: Corwin, 2007), 133–153.

3. Wikipedia, s.v. "Richard Fenno," last modified August 7, 2015, https://en.wikipedia.org/wiki/Richard_Fenno.

4. John Teasdale, Mark Williams, and Zindel Segal, *The Mindful Way Workbook: An 8-Week Program to Free Yourself from Depression and Emotional Distress* (New York: Guilford, 2014), 7.

5. Zindel V. Segal, J. Mark G. Williams, and John D. Teasdale, *Mindfulness-Based Cognitive Therapy for Depression*, 2nd ed. (New York: Guilford, 2013).

6. Susan M. Orsillo and Lizabeth Roemer, *The Mindful Way Through Anxiety: Break Free from Chronic Worry and Reclaim Your Life* (New York:

Guilford, 2011); Marsha M. Linehan, *Cognitive-Behavioral Treatment of Borderline Personality Disorder* (New York: Guilford, 1993); Jon Kabat-Zinn, *Full Catastrophe Living: Using the Wisdom of Your Body and Mind to Face Stress, Pain, and Illness* (New York: Delta, 1990). Also see Center for Mindfulness in Medicine, Health Care, and Society, "Mobilize Your Own Inner Resources for Learning, Growing, and Healing," accessed December 14, 2015, www.umassmed.edu/cfm/stress-reduction/.

7. Teasdale, Williams, and Segal, *Mindful Way*, 30.
8. Richard J. Davidson and Sona Dimidjian, "The Emergence of Mindfulness in Basic and Clinical Psychological Science," *American Psychologist* 70, no. 7 (October 2015).
9. Arianna Huffington, "Mindfulness a Presence at Davos," *Huffington Post*, January 30, 2013, http://www.arcamax.com/politics/fromtheleft/ariannahuffington/s-1271945.
10. Focusing was first described by philosopher and psychotherapist Eugene Gendlin as an attention-based method that enhances our ability to connect deeply with our inner selves. See Eugene T. Gendlin, *Focusing*, 25th anniv. ed. (New York: Bantam, 2003). It helps us move forward by bringing a caring awareness to our in-the-moment "felt sense" of a situation, particularly our bodily sensations. In focusing, we discover—and build on—new self-knowledge, which often lies hidden and fuzzy below the conceptual level, and bring it into focus.

I have been particularly inspired by two of Gendlin's students: Ann Weiser Cornell and David Rome. Cornell (alongside Barbara McGavin) has been doing groundbreaking work that emphasizes the relationship between what they call "self-in-presence" (a dimension of us with the capacity for deep listening and compassion) and our inner parts that are often in conflict. Self-in-presence can help create a space for the felt sense to emerge and for genuine change to occur. See Focusing Resources home page, accessed March 15, 2016, www.focusingresources.com.

David Rome offers a compelling integration of focusing and mindfulness: "Meditation is wonderful for stepping away from the speed and complexities of everyday life and finding refuge in a calmer more spacious quality of mind, but it can be insufficient to bring light to the deeper roots of feeling." In Rome's view, mindfulness-based practices are not always the best tool for practical problem solving, given their emphasis on noting what arises and then letting it go. He believes focusing provides a "simple but powerful means to bridge from sitting meditation practice to the nitty-gritty of everyday life." David I. Rome, *Your Body Knows the Answer: Using Your Felt Sense to Solve Problems, Effect Change and Liberate Creativity* (Boston: Shambhala, 2014), xiv.

IFS is the brainchild of psychologist Richard Schwartz, who began as a family therapist using systems theory and then discovered through clinical work that his theories could be adapted to the inner lives of clients. Like focusing, IFS is beginning to gain strong advocates among those with deep roots in Buddhist traditions. For example, meditation teacher Jack Engler finds IFS helpful: "I've also found IFS very compatible with mindfulness and have made it part of my daily meditation practice." Jack Engler, "An Introduction to IFS," in *IFS: Internal Family Systems, New Dimensions*, ed. Martha Sweeney and Ellen L. Ziskind (New York: Routledge, 2013), xxv.

Although the details differ, IFS and focusing both emphasize working with troubled inner parts of us that can be in conflict. Like focusing, IFS also helps us show up as more than nonjudgmental observers of our experiences. Indeed, Schwartz believes each of us has at our core a self that "contains the compassion, perspective, confidence, and vision required to lead both internal and external life harmoniously and sensitively. It is not just a passing observing state, but can be an actor in both inner and outer dramas." Richard C. Schwartz, *Internal Family Systems Therapy* (New York: Guilford, 1995), 40; Center for Self Leadership, home page, accessed March 15, 2016, www.selfleadership.org.

11. In 2015, the name of the Inner Strengths of Successful Leaders workshop was changed from ISSL to BISL (Building the Inner Strengths of Leaders).

Chapter 4

1. Viktor E. Frankl, quoted in BrainyQuote.com, accessed January 7, 2016, www.brainyquote.com/quotes/quotes/v/viktorefr160380.html.

Chapter 5

1. Steven C. Hayes, Kirk D. Strosahl, and Kelly G. Wilson, *Acceptance and Commitment Therapy: The Process and Practice of Mindful Change*, 2nd

ed. (New York: Guilford, 2012), chap. 11.

2. Viktor E. Frankl, *Man's Search for Meaning: An Introduction to Logotherapy* (New York: Simon & Schuster, 1984).

3. Carolyn Gregoire, "This Man Faced Unimaginable Suffering, and Then Wrote the Definitive Book About Happiness," *Huffington Post*, August 18, 2014, www.huffingtonpost.com/2014/02/04/this-book-youve-probably-_n_4705123.html.

4. Ronald Heifetz, Alexander Grashow, and Marty Linsky, *The Practice of Adaptive Leadership: Tools and Tactics for Changing Your Organization and the World* (Boston: Harvard Business Press, 2009), 38–39.

5. For a discussion of value conflicts, see Russ Harris, "How to Resolve Values Conflicts," part 1 (2015), "I'm Learning ACT," web page, www.actmindfully.com.au/upimages/How_To_Resolve_Values_Conflicts.pdf?utm_source=Synced+from+ACT+Mindfully+2&utm_c=df36a a3f79-.

6. Some sources attribute this quote to Hunter S. Thompson.

7. Inspired by Russ Harris, *ACT Made Simple: An Easy-to-Read Primer on Acceptance and Commitment Therapy* (Oakland, CA: New Harbinger, 2009), chap. 11.

8. In September 2015, the Massachusetts Institute of Technology announced an interesting app for identifying and acting on your personal values. See Dalai Lama Center for Ethics and Transformative Values, "Mitra: Track What Matters Most," application, accessed January 8, 2016, https://itunes.apple.com/us/app/mitra-track-what-matters-most/id1020233743?mt=8.

9. Matthew McKay, John P. Forsyth, and Georg H. Eifert, *Your Life on Purpose: How to Find What Matters and Create the Life You Want* (Oakland, CA: New Harbinger, 2010), 119.

Chapter 6

1. Jon Kabat-Zinn, *Mindfulness for Beginners: Reclaiming the Present Moment—and Your Life* (Boulder, CO: Sounds True, 2012), 1.

2. Antoine Lutz, Amishi P. Jha, John D. Dunne, and Clifford D. Saron, "Investigating the Phenomenological Matrix of Mindfulness-Related Practices from a Neurocognitive Perspective," *American Psychologist* 70, no. 7 (2015): 632–658.

3. Steve Bradt, "Wandering Mind Not a Happy Mind," *Harvard Gazette*, November 11, 2010, http://news.harvard.edu/gazette/story/2010/11/wandering-mind-not-a-happy-mind.

4. William James, *The Principles of Psychology* (New York: H. Holt, 1890), 463.

5. Christina C. Feldman, *The Buddhist Path to Simplicity: Spiritual Practice for Everyday Life* (London: Harper/Collins, 2001), 167.

6. Kabat-Zinn, *Mindfulness for Beginners*.

7. Susan M. Pollak, Thomas Pedulla, and Ronald D. Siegel, *Sitting Together: Essential Skills for Mindfulness-Based Psychotherapy* (New York: Guilford, 2014), 67–69, 142–143.

8. Alexandra Sifferlin, "Washing Dishes Is a Really Great Stress Reliever, Science Says," *Time*, September 30, 2015, http://time.com/4056280/washing-dishes-stress-relief-mindfulness/.

9. Washington Mindfulness Community, Mindfulness Bell (app), Washington Mindfulness Community, Takoma Park, MD, accessed January 9, 2016, www.mindfulnessdc.org/bell/index.html. Also, throughout this book, I emphasize informal practices, many of which come from mindfulness- and acceptance-based psychotherapies, such as acceptance and commitment therapy. In particular, I'm indebted to the imaginative work of Russ Harris. For more information on this therapy, see Association for Contextual Behavioral Science, home page, accessed January 9, 2016, https://contextualscience.org.

10. Rick Hanson, "How to Grow the Good in Your Brain," *Greater Good: The Science of a Meaningful Life*, University of California, Berkeley, September 24, 2013, http://greatergood.berkeley.edu/article/item/how_to_grow_the_good_in_your_brain.

11. The focus here is on a central dimension of rumination—namely, obsessing about the past and future. Rumination is also marked by other unhelpful mental habits discussed in later chapters (e.g., identifying with your upsets, the absence of self-compassion). Consequently, step 2 of my dance, yield to now, goes hand-in-hand with other steps in addressing the various dimensions of rumination.

12. Joseph Goldstein, *Mindfulness: A Practical Guide to Awakening* (Boulder, CO: Sounds True, 2013), 359.

13. A similar argument can be made about disrupting the other components of the three Rs—resistance and self-rebuke.

14. See Goldstein, *Mindfulness*, 395, for a discussion of "cowboy dharma."

15. Daniel Goleman, *Focus: The Hidden Driver of Excellence* (New York: Harper, 2013), 4. Also see Daniel Goleman, "Why Leaders Need a Triple Focus," *Greater Good: The Science of a Meaningful Life*,

University of California, Berkeley, January 21, 2014, http://greater-good.berkeley.edu/article/item/why_leaders_need_a_triple_focus.

16. For a good summary of the benefits of mindfulness at work, see Peter Jaret, "Why We Need Mindfulness at Work," Greater Good: The Science of a Meaningful Life, University of California, Berkeley, November 4, 2015, http://greatergood.berkeley.edu/article/item/why_we_need_mindfulness_at_work?utm_source=GGSC+Newsletter+-+November++2015&utm_campaign=GG+Newsletter++-+November+2015&utm_medium=email.

17. My thanks to Jeffrey Young for this observation.

18. Paul E. Flaxman, Frank W. Bond, and Fredrik Livheim, *The Mindful and Effective Employee: An Acceptance and Commitment Therapy Training Manual for Improving Well-Being and Performance* (Oakland, CA: New Harbinger, 2013), 175.

Chapter 7

1. My perspective in this chapter has been influenced mainly by readings on mindfulness, but two other complementary lines of work bear mention: Ethan Kross and Ozlem Ayduk, "Making Meaning out of Negative Experiences by Self-Distancing," Current Directions in Psychological Science 20, no. 3 (2011): 187–191; and Adrian Wells, *Metacognitive Therapy for Anxiety and Depression* (New York: Guilford, 2009).

2. India.Arie, "I Am Light," accessed February 9, 2016, www.azlyrics.com/lyrics/indiaarie/iamlight.html.

3. Steven C. Hayes, Kirk D. Strosahl, and Kelly G. Wilson, *Acceptance and Commitment Therapy: The Process and Practice of Mindful Change*, 2nd ed. (New York: Guilford, 2012), 259.

4. Matthieu Ricard, *Why Meditate? Working with Thoughts and Emotions*, trans. Sherab Chödzin Kohn (Carlsbad, CA: Hay House, 2010), 114–115.

5. Russ Harris, *ACT Made Simple: An Easy-to-Read Primer on Acceptance and Commitment Therapy* (Oakland, CA: New Harbinger, 2009), 20–21.

6. Heidi Fischbach, "Alone in the Cafeteria," Heidi's Table (blog), October 19, 2015, http://heidistable.com/alone-in-cafeteria/.

7. David I. Rome, *Your Body Knows the Answer: Using Your FELT SENSE to Solve Problems, Effect Change, and Liberate Creativity* (Boston: Shambhala, 2014), 31.

8. Arthur J. Deikman, *The Observing Self: Mysticism and Psychotherapy* (Boston: Beacon, 1982), 108.

9. Jon Kabat-Zinn, "Mindfulness of Sounds and Thoughts," segment in *Guided Meditation Practices* (CD-ROM), at 10:34, in *The Mindful Way Through Depression: Freeing Yourself from Chronic Unhappiness*, by J. Mark G. Williams, John D. Teasdale, Zindel V. Segal, and Jon Kabat-Zinn (New York: Guilford Press, 2007).

10. This exercise was adapted from Harris, *ACT Made Simple*, 177.

11. These exercises were inspired by ibid., 113–114.

12. Ann Weiser Cornell, *Focusing in Clinical Practice: The Essence of Change* (New York: Norton, 2013), 93; Ann Weiser Cornell, *The Radical Acceptance of Everything: Living a Focusing Life* (Berkeley, CA: Calluna Press, 2005). Also see Ann Weiser Cornell, *Get Bigger Than What's Bugging You*, a free online course that you can access at Focusing Resources, accessed February 10, 2016, https://tj255.infusionsoft .com/app/form/4738d781e8c12fdcf27ab53aaa304c5d.

13. Jack Kornfield and Joseph Goldstein, "What Makes Us Free," *Shambhula Sun Magazine*, January 2014, 41.

14. John Teasdale, Mark Williams, and Zindel Segal, *The Mindful Way Workbook: An 8-Week Program to Free Yourself from Depression and Emotional Distress* (New York: Guilford, 2014), 24.

15. Rick Hanson, *Hardwiring Happiness: The New Brain Science of Contentment, Calm, and Confidence* (New York: Harmony, 2013), 7–8.

Chapter 8

1. In the field, people use the acronym ACT interchangeably with acceptance and commitment training.

2. Inspired by Russ Harris, *ACT Made Simple: An Easy-to-Read Primer on Acceptance and Commitment Therapy* (Oakland, CA: New Harbinger, 2009), 15.

3. Zindel V. Segal, J. Mark G. Williams, and John D. Teasdale, *Mindfulness-Based Cognitive Therapy for Depression: A New Approach to Preventing Relapse*, 2nd ed. (New York: Guilford, 2012), 290.

4. Susan M. Orsillo and Lizabeth Roemer, *The Mindful Way Through Anxiety: Break Free from Chronic Worry and Reclaim Your Life* (New York: Guilford, 2011), 171.

5. Jalaluddin Rumi, "The Guest House" in *The Essential Rumi*, new expanded ed., trans. Coleman Barks, with John Moyne, A. J. Arberry, and Reynold Nicholson (New York: HarperCollins, 2010).

6. Steven C. Hayes, with Spencer Smith, *Get Out of Your Mind and Into Your Life: The New Acceptance and Commitment Therapy* (Oakland, CA: New Harbinger, 2005), 7.
7. The metaphor description was inspired by Steven C. Hayes, Kirk D. Strosahl, and Kelly G. Wilson, *Acceptance and Commitment Therapy: The Process and Practice of Mindful Change* (New York: Guilford, 1999), 248.
8. Shauna L. Shapiro and Linda E. Carlson, *The Art and Science of Mindfulness: Integrating Mindfulness into Psychology and the Helping Professions* (Washington, DC: American Psychological Association, 2009), 5–6.
9. Adapted from Susan M. Pollak, Thomas Pedulla and Ronald D. Siegel, *Sitting Together: Essential Skills for Mindfulness-Based Psychotherapy* (New York: Guilford, 2014), 158.
10. Danna Faulds, *Go In and In* (Greenville, VA: Peaceable Kingdom Books, 2002), 25.
11. Harris, *ACT Made Simple*, 137.
12. Joseph Ciarrochi, Ann Bailey, and Russ Harris, *The Weight Escape: How to Stop Dieting and Start Living* (Boston: Shambhala, 2014), 50–51.
13. This exercise was inspired by Caitlin Ferriter, "Crying Baby on the Plane" in *The Big Book of ACT Metaphors: A Practitioner's Guide to Experiential Exercises & Metaphors in Acceptance & Commitment Therapy*, ed. Jill A. Stoddard and Niloofar Afari (Oakland, CA: New Harbinger, 2014), 55.

Chapter 9

1. In writing this chapter, I'd like to particularly note the contribution of Zindel V. Segal, J Mark G. Williams and John D. Teasdale, "How Can I Best Take Care of Myself," in *Mindfulness-Based Cognitive Therapy for Depression: A New Approach for Preventing Relapse* (New York: Guilford, 2002), 269–290.
2. Mark Williams and Danny Penman, *Mindfulness: An Eight-Week Plan for Finding Peace in a Frantic World* (New York: Rodale, 2011), 213.
3. Ibid., 214.
4. Rick Hanson, *Hardwiring Happiness: The New Brain Science of Contentment, Calm, and Confidence* (New York: Harmony, 2013), dust jacket.
5. Ibid.
6. Nutritious eating and regular exercise are important elements of self-care, of course, and they are well documented elsewhere. For an excellent resource that combines the science of nutrition and

exercise along with the practice of mindfulness, see Thich Nhat Hanh and Lilian Cheung, *Savor: Mindful Eating, Mindful Life* (New York: Harper One, 2010).

7. John Teasdale, Mark Williams, and Zindel Segal, *The Mindful Way Workbook: An 8-Week Program to Free Yourself from Depression and Emotional Distress* (New York, Guilford: 2014), 171, 172, 178. Emphasis in original.

8. National Sleep Foundation, "Napping," accessed February 10, 2016, https://sleepfoundation.org/sleep-topics/napping.

9. Arianna Huffington, *Thrive: The Third Metric to Redirecting Success and Creating a Life of Well-Being, Wisdom, and Wonder* (New York: Harmony, 2014).

10. Benson-Henry Institute for Mind Body Medicine, "Mind Body Medicine: New Science and Best Practices to Meet Public Health Challenges, October 20–23, 2016," CME Trainings, accessed February 10, 2016, http://bensonhenryinstitute.org/professional-training/live-cme.

11. Herbert Benson and William Proctor, *Relaxation Revolution: Enhancing Your Personal Health Through the Science and Genetics of Mind Body Healing* (New York: Scribner, 2010), 9.

12. Heidi Fischbach, "Alone in the Cafeteria," *Heidi's Table* (blog), October 19, 2015, http://heidistable.com/alone-in-cafeteria/.

13. Williams and Penman, *Mindfulness*, 220.

14. Esther M. Sternberg, *Healing Spaces: The Science of Place and Well-Being* (Cambridge, MA: Harvard University Press, 2009). Also see Esther Sternberg, "The Science of Healing Places," in *On Being with Krista Tippitt*, www.onbeing.org/program/the-science-of-healing-places/4856.

15. Lyndall Gordon, *Virginia Woolf: A Writer's Life* (New York: Norton, 2001), 250.

16. Mary Oliver, *Thirst* (Boston: Beacon, 2006), 4.

17. Mark Bielang, "Chuang Tzu's 'Flight from the Shadow,'" in *Teaching with Heart: Poetry That Speaks to the Courage to Teach*, ed. Sam M. Intrator and Megan Scribner (San Francisco: Jossey-Bass, 2014), 154. In November 2015, Bielang was superintendent of schools in Portage, Michigan.

18. David Steindl-Rast, "A Beautiful Day," video, *Gratefulness.org, A Network for Grateful Living*, 2007, www.gratefulness.org/resource/a-good-day.

19. Hanson, *Hardwiring Happiness*, 28.
20. Ibid., dust jacket.
21. Ibid., 70 and 74. For the details and nuances of how to take in the good, and for the convincing science behind this powerful practice, I recommend Hanson, *Hardwiring Happiness*.
22. Nancy Shute, "Take Your Dog to the Office and Stress Less," *Shots: Health News from NPR*, updated July 3, 2012, www.npr.org/sections/health-shots/2012/03/30/149684409.

Chapter 10

1. Kristin Neff, *Self-Compassion: Stop Beating Yourself Up and Leave Insecurity Behind* (New York: Morrow, 2011), 121–122.
2. Ann Weiser Cornell, "Get Bigger Than What's Bugging You," *Focusing Resources*, 2010, www.focusingresources.com/?portfolio=get-bigger-than-whats-bugging-you.
3. Kristin Neff, *Self-Compassion* home page, accessed February 2, 2016, http://selfcompassion.org.
4. Zindel V. Segal, J. Mark G. Williams, and John D. Teasdale, *Mindfulness-Based Cognitive Therapy for Depression*, 2nd ed. (New York: Guilford, 2013), 137.
5. Paul Gilbert, introduction to *The Compassionate Mind Approach to Overcoming Anxiety: Using Compassion Focused Therapy*, by Dennis Tirch (London: Robinson, 2012), xv.
6. Paul Gilbert, *The Compassionate Mind: A New Approach to Life's Challenges* (Oakland, CA: Harbinger, 2009); Paul Gilbert, *Compassion Focused Therapy: Distinctive Features* (London: Routledge, 2010).
7. Kristin Neff, "The Three Elements of Self-Compassion," *Self-Compassion* website, 2016, http://self-compassion.org/the-three-elements-of-self-compassion-2.
8. Christopher K. Germer, "Mindful Self-Compassion," accessed February 10, 2016, www.mindfulselfcompassion.org. In particular, see Christopher K. Germer, *The Mindful Way to Self-Compassion: Freeing Yourself from Destructive Thoughts and Emotions* (New York: Guilford, 2009).
9. Matthieu Ricard, Antoine Lutz, and Richard J. Davidson, "Mind of the Meditator," *Scientific American* 311, no. 5 (November 2014): 44.
10. Pema Chödrön, "Turn Your Thinking Upside Down," *The Lion's Roar: Buddhist Wisdom for Your Life*, May 1, 2007, www.lionsroar.com/turn-your-thinking-upside-down.

11. Kristin Neff and Christopher K. Germer, "Being Kind to Yourself: The Science of Self-Compassion," in *Compassion: Bridging Theory and Practice—A Multimedia Book*, ed. Tania Singer and Matthias Bolz (Leipzig, Germany: Max-Planck Institute, 2013), 291.

12. Robyn Griggs Lawrence, *The Wabi-Sabi House: The Japanese Art of Imperfect Beauty* (New York: Random House, 2004), 17.

13. Ann Weiser Cornell, "Tips for Challenging Times: 7 Little Words," video, *Focusing Resources*, accessed February 10, 2016, http://focusing resources.com/tips-for-challenging-times-7-little-words/, tells the story of how her life was changed when she first read seven little words: "You can be the way you are."

14. Kristin Neff, "Self-Compassion Publications," *Self-Compassion* website, accessed February 10, 2016, http://self-compassion.org/the-research. Also see Germer, "Mindful Self-Compassion."

15. Christopher K. Germer, "Resources: Handouts," *Mindful Self-Compassion* website, accessed February 10, 2016, www.mindfulself compassion.org/resources_handouts.php.

16. Ibid.

17. Eden Steinberg, ed., *The Pocket Pema Chödrön* (Boston: Shambhala, 2008), 21.

18. Jack Kornfield, "How to Do Metta," *Lion's Roar: Buddhist Wisdom for Your Life*, August 11, 2015, www.lionsroar.com/how-to-do-metta-january-2014. For an older discourse on loving-kindness—a discussion that remains remarkably fresh today—see Sharon Salzberg, *Lovingkindness: The Revolutionary Art of Happiness* (Boston: Shambhala, 2004).

Chapter 11

1. Joseph Goldstein, *Shambhala Sun Magazine*, January 2014, 9.

2. Katharine Graham, *Personal History* (New York: Random House, 1997), 550.

3. Linda A. Hill, *Becoming a Manager: How New Managers Master the Challenges of Leadership* (Boston: Harvard Business School, 2003), 175.

4. Barry C. Jentz and Jerome T. Murphy, "Embracing Confusion: What Leaders Do When They Don't Know What to Do," *Phi Delta Kappan* 86 no. 5 (January 2005): 363.

5. Ibid.

6. Morris Freilich, "The Natural Triad in Kinship and Complex Systems," *American Sociological Review* 29 no. 4 (August 1964): 529–540.

7. Matt Licata and Jeff Foster, "Healers, Therapists, Friends, and Lovers!," in *A Healing Space* (blog), December 13, 2014, http://alovinghealingspace.blogspot.com/2014/12/healers-therapists-friends-and-lovers.html.

Chapter 12

1. Dan Harris, *10% Happier: How I Tamed the Voice in My Head, Reduced Stress Without Losing My Edge, and Found Self-Help That Actually Works—A True Story* (New York: HarperCollins, 2014).
2. The reflection was written by Sharon Pavelda and Randall Mullins. In his November 18, 2015, email giving permission, Mullins wrote, "By the way, it turned out that I did not have ALS. It was cancer in the tongue. I am now almost 3 years after surgery and doing well."

Postlude

1. Oriah Mountain Dreamer, *The Dance: Moving to the Deep Rhythms of Your Life* (New York: HarperCollins), 2001, xi.

ACKNOWLEDGMENTS

WRITING THIS BOOK vividly reminds me how much we all depend on others for inspiration, insight, feedback, and emotional support. It also reminds me that most good ideas are old ideas—and that much of what we know about education comes from the wisdom of practice. I welcome this opportunity to acknowledge with humility the scholars who have preceded me and the educators on the ground who make such a difference without receiving the recognition they deserve. It's also an honor to thank publicly many others for their varied contributions to this book—and for making such a big difference in my life.

First of all, my heartfelt thanks to the colleagues, students, mentors, leaders, and friends who offered feedback on numerous drafts—and to others who helped me clarify my thinking, regain my perspective, or just stay afloat: Deena Barlev, Andy Barry, Ari Betof, Richard Brown, Tom Champion, David Cohen, Brooke Dodson-Lavelle, Rosemary Downer, Alistair Finlay, Heidi Fischbach, Brent Forester, Kristin Foster, Deborah Garson, Patricia Graham, David Hirshberg, Tish Jennings, Barry Jentz, Lucy Kim, Judi Knowles, Mary Jo Kramer, Ellen Matheson, Grady McGonagill, Lois Miller, Richard Murnane, Kirsten Olson, Alisa Pascale, Kelly Pickle, Barbara Ray, Holly Rollins, David Rome, Pamela Seigle, Hugh Silbaugh, Wendy Slattebo, Janet Solyntjes, Ernie Squeglia, Robert Suntay, Mark Wilding, Rona Wilensky, and my fellow meditators at the Cambridge Insight Meditation Center. Special thanks to Jeff Young for his great insight and perceptive suggestions on reading the penultimate draft, and Tom Rocha and Patricia Boyd for their superb editorial assistance.

My thanks to members of my family who bigheartedly offered encouragement, stories, research assistance, editorial ideas, or a place to hang out without being disturbed: Marcella Agerholm, Susan Agrue, Cindy and Mark Guy, Jean Murphy, and Martha Murphy.

Over the course of my writing, four multiyear group activities have been especially influential. My thanks go to numerous people:

The wonderful students in my courses on leadership at the Harvard Graduate School of Education sharpened my thinking with their questions and insights. Special thanks to Metta McGarvey, my teaching assistant at the time, who introduced me to mindfulness and was instrumental in introducing it into our classes. Metta helped change the direction of my work in ways for which I'm eternally grateful.

The faculty, participants, and staff of Inner Strengths of Successful Leaders, an annual workshop sponsored by Programs in Professional Education at the Harvard Graduate School of Education. (Cocreated by Metta and me, the workshop now continues under Metta's leadership with a new name, Building the Inner Strengths of Leaders.) My thanks to key staff—Mary O'Neill, Madeline Tarabelli, Josh Williamson, and Joe Zolner. And thanks to an incredible faculty over the years: Herbert Benson, Chris Germer, Rick Hanson, Liz Roemer, and Diana Chapman Walsh. Special thanks to Chris, who regularly astonishes me with his wisdom and kindness.

The members and staff of the Leadership Council, Contemplative Teaching and Learning Initiative at the Garrison Institute were a remarkable group of scholars, government officials, and school practitioners who shaped my thinking through their wisdom and passionate recounting of their experiences.

The members and staff of the Ethics, Education, and Human Development Advisory Board at the Mind and Life Institute were an intellectually diverse and stimulating group that opened my mind to a wide range of new ideas and important issues.

I also thank a number of additional scribblers—most are cited in the book—who have been particularly influential in helping me better understand the inner lives of leaders. They include Richard Ackerman, Ruth Baer, Josh Bartok, Ezra Bayda, Sylvia Boorstein, Tara Brach, Helene Brenner, Trish Broderick, Mirabai Bush, Pema Chödrön, Ann Weiser Cornell, Georg Eifert, Jack Engler, John Forsyth, Viktor Frankl, Gene Gendlin, Paul Gilbert, Joseph Goldstein, Daniel Goleman, Susan Greenland, Thich Nhat Hanh, Russ Harris, Tobin Hart, Steve Hayes, Ron Heifetz, Jon Kabat-Zinn, Jack Kornfield, His Holiness the Dalai Lama, Linda Lantieri, Marsha Linehan, Pat Maslin-Ostrowski, Barbara McGavin, Kristin Neff, Matthieu Ricard, Sharon Salzberg, Richard Schwartz, Dan Siegel, Ron Siegel, Kirk Strosahl, Mark Williams, and Kelly Wilson.

My thanks to the Pforzheimer Foundation and the Spencer Foundation for two small grants that were instrumental in getting this project under way. And thanks to the staff at the Harvard Education Press for so ably bringing this book to completion.

Finally, I never would have finished this book without the inspiration, encouragement, and help of four amazing women: Pamela Brooke, a distinguished writer, masterful editor, and longtime friend, helped me find both my voice and a way forward when I was floundering. Caroline Chauncey, the Harvard Ed Press's chief editor, generously offered sage advice with grace and compassion—and set a deadline at just the right time. Nancy Murphy, my mother, the brightest light in the room even as she grew blind and deaf, showed me what it really means to dance in the rain. And Susan Murphy, my dear wife and best friend, editor, and advisor for almost fifty years, inspires me daily as she bravely deals with Alzheimer's disease and is guided by her mantra: "Courage, compassion, and good humor."

A deep bow to all of you.

ABOUT THE AUTHOR

JEROME T. MURPHY is the Harold Howe II Professor of Education Emeritus and Dean Emeritus at the Harvard Graduate School of Education. His current teaching and research focuses on the inner life of education leaders and how to find meaning and vitality in the midst of stress and strain.

A graduate of Columbia College and Columbia Teachers College and coming from a family of proud teachers, Murphy started his career with two rewarding years as a public school math teacher. He then unexpectedly got a job working for the federal government as part of the War on Poverty. He was part of a team that helped develop the Elementary and Secondary Education Act of 1965, and he later spent an unforgettable year as the Associate Director of the White House Fellows Program and the Associate Staff Director of the National Advisory Council on the Education of Disadvantaged Children. During these heady days in Washington, his eyes were opened to the nuances of leadership as he observed up close how political leaders and dedicated civil servants actually engage in principled politics in the pursuit of noble ends.

Shortly after Richard Nixon was elected president, Murphy moved on to become a doctoral student at the Harvard Graduate School of Education and has been there ever since, but for a delightful two years as a Visiting Professor at the Penn Graduate School of Education.

Drawing on his seven years in public schooling and government service, Murphy turned his attention to studying and writing about the everyday reality of how things actually work in education. He became a specialist in the politics of education, with a focus on government policy, program implementation and evaluation, organizational leadership, and qualitative methodology.

Murphy conducted some of the earliest studies of the implementation of the Great Society education programs and the role of the states in educational policy and governance; he contributed to novel data-collection techniques in educational evaluation. Along the way, he has written books and articles about these topics as well as about schools of education, about the lives of education leaders, and about the changing roles of school superintendents and chief state school officers. Murphy has also examined educational policy and practices in Australia, China, Colombia, England, Japan, and South Africa and has given presentations at research meetings in Denmark, Israel, Norway, Russia, Saudi Arabia, Sweden, and Thailand.

For almost twenty years, Murphy was a full-time administrator at the Harvard Graduate School of Education, first as Associate Dean from 1982 to 1991 and then as Dean from 1992 to 2001. As Dean, Murphy led the development of new initiatives in learning technologies, arts education, neuroscience, and school leadership. He also led a capital campaign, which almost doubled the hoped-for goal, and was honored at Harvard with an endowed chair named after him.

Throughout his career, Murphy has aspired to live up to a definition he once heard describing a professor—namely, someone who "thinks otherwise" and challenges prevailing views about what's important and what deserves attention. In his teaching, he urged students to think otherwise by being troublemakers, stirring things up and fighting for their values—just like Nelson Mandela, whose given name in his native language is "troublemaker." In his research, Murphy thought otherwise by writing about policy implementation when research focused mainly on policy development; about state government when researchers were preoccupied with the federal government; about qualitative methods as a complement to quantitative methods; about the unheroic side of leadership, when bigger-than-life leaders were lionized; and, most recently, about the inner lives of education leaders when their training programs and supporting research studies often overlook the inside-the-skin challenges of leadership.

INDEX

children, 19, 28
Chinese finger trap metaphor, 128–129
Chödrön, Pema, 181, 188
chronic stress, 151
Churchill, Winston, 150
cognitive therapy, 46–47
comfort zone, 42, 63–64
commitment, 73
common humanity, 179, 211
compassion, 9, 171–174, 179–180, 184, 203, 208, 210–211
  See also self-compassion
compassion-focused therapy (CFT), 178
complexity, 2
confusion, 76, 124, 198
consciousness, 103–105
Cornell, Ann Weiser, 117, 174
corporate face, 20
courage, 64, 76, 222
coworkers, relationships with, 99
credibility, 34
curiosity, 85
"CVS Morning Pause" exercise, 164–165

dancing in rain metaphor, 4–7, 39, 40, 42
Darwin, Charles, 75
Davies, Timothy, 20
decision-making, 20, 34, 73
Deikman, Arthur, 111–112
direct experience, 85
direction, sense of, 208
discomfort
  concealing, 196–198
  opening up to, 123–143
  reactions to, 23–35, 40
  welcoming, 126–127
disentangling from upsets, 9, 41, 101–121

distance, 34
distractions, 99
dogs, 166

education leaders
  See also leaders; leadership
  effectiveness of, 8
  external lives of, 8
  inner lives of, 8
  pressures facing, 2–3, 11, 15–21, 41–42, 50–51
  self-compassion and, 181–182
Edwards, Dan, 6
effectiveness, 6, 8
Eifert, Georg, 24–25
emotional blocks, 72
emotional challenges
  reactions to, 23–35
  types of, 17–21
emotional discomfort, 3
emotional exhaustion, 180
emotional regulation, 24–25
emotions/feelings
  allowing and accepting your, 123–143
  displaying warmth, 203–205
  expressing, 9, 41, 193–212
  handling upsetting, 107–114
  indirectly expressing, 202–203
  intense, 137–138
  naming your, 199–202
  observing your, 108
  revealing, 196–200
  stepping back from, 110–113
  unexpected events and, 205–211
  welcoming stance toward, 126–127
empathy, 99, 179–180, 203, 210
empathy fatigue, 180
Entangled Mind, 108, 119, 121
Epstein, Mark, 18
escape, 26